Flip the Switch

Achieve Extraordinary Things with Simple Changes to How you Think

Jez Rose

CAPSTONE
A Wiley Brand

This edition first published 2016

© 2016 Jez Rose

Registered office

John Wiley and Sons Ltd, The Atrium, Southern Gate, Chichester, West Sussex, PO19 8SQ, United Kingdom

For details of our global editorial offices, for customer services and for information about how to apply for permission to reuse the copyright material in this book please see our website at www.wiley.com.

The right of the author to be identified as the author of this work has been asserted in accordance with the Copyright, Designs and Patents Act 1988.

Wiley publishes in a variety of print and electronic formats and by print-on-demand. Some material included with standard print versions of this book may not be included in e-books or in print-on-demand. If this book refers to media such as a CD or DVD that is not included in the version you purchased, you may download this material at http://booksupport.wiley.com. For more information about Wiley products, visit www.wiley.com.

Designations used by companies to distinguish their products are often claimed as trademarks. All brand names and product names used in this book and on its cover are trade names, service marks, trademarks or registered trademarks of their respective owners. The publisher and the book are not associated with any product or vendor mentioned in this book. None of the companies referenced within the book have endorsed the book.

Limit of Liability/Disclaimer of Warranty: While the publisher and author have used their best efforts in preparing this book, they make no representations or warranties with respect to the accuracy or completeness of the contents of this book and specifically disclaim any implied warranties of merchantability or fitness for a particular purpose. It is sold on the understanding that the publisher is not engaged in rendering professional services and neither the publisher nor the author shall be liable for damages arising herefrom. If professional advice or other expert assistance is required, the services of a competent professional should be sought.

Library of Congress Cataloging-in-Publication Data

Names: Rose, Jez, author.
Title: Flip the switch : achieve extraordinary things with simple changes to how you think / Jez Rose.
Description: Chichester, West Sussex, United Kingdom : John Wiley & Sons, Inc., 2016.
Identifiers: LCCN 2015048909 (print) I LCCN 2016005039 (ebook) I ISBN 9780857086792 (paperback)
Subjects: LCSH: Change (Psychology) I Attitude change. I Thought and thinking. I Success. I BISAC: SELF-HELP / Motivational & Inspirational.
Classification: LCC BF637.C4 R67 2016 (print) I LCC BF637.C4 (ebook) I DDC 158.1–dc23
LC record available at http://lccn.loc.gov/2015048909

A catalogue record for this book is available from the British Library.

ISBN 978-0-857-08679-2 (pbk)
ISBN 978-0-857-08680-8 (ebk) ISBN 978-0-857-08682-2 (ebk)

Cover Design: Wiley
Cover Image: © ISebyl/Shutterstock

Set in 12/15pt Sabon by Aptara Inc., New Delhi, India
Printed in Great Britain by TJ International Ltd, Padstow, Cornwall, UK

For Gwendoline Pearl Cunliffe - Grandma.

Contents

Foreword

Jez is an expert in human behaviour and more specifically in how to get people to change their behaviour for the better, whilst understanding why we do the things we do. I know what it's like to have little available time when you are focused on driving your own higher performance and achieving goals and Jez does this not only for himself but for organisations and individuals including celebrities and nobility, all over the world.

Flip the Switch is at times hilarious but the message is a useful one and for some, it may well be the awakening they need to achieve great things at work or indeed in their personal life. Whatever your reason for reading this, I suggest you begin by embracing the challenges that stand in your way – there's absolutely no point in crying over spilt milk; it's happened. It's done. I share Jez's belief that every human being is capable of achieving extraordinary things, if only we understand that the key is to learn from our perceived failures – and then keep going.

Sir Ranulph Fiennes
"The world's greatest living explorer"
[*The Guinness Book of Records*] and recipient
of multiple awards and honorariums

Introduction

....

"Between stimulus and response there is a space. In that space is our power to choose our response. In our response lies our growth and our freedom."

Dr. Viktor E. Frankl, from *Man's Search for Meaning*

When I first read Dr. Frankl's take on the behavioural void between those things which cause us to respond and the physical response itself, I went physically cold. He had articulated so succinctly what I had been questioning and worrying over for a long time: that our ability to actively choose our behaviour seemed to be wasting away. If that were the case, we would be in danger of becoming a species of drones; instantly responding to stimulus without due care or consideration. Whether at work or at home, the implications of that are significant.

As a speaker and behaviourist working with organizations worldwide, I've seen over the past twelve years how individuals in organizations are often faced with obstruction when it comes to personal and professional development that is behavioural in nature. This is because in many cases reflection and thoughtfulness, indeed the very consideration of behaviour, is viewed as inertia. However, the purpose of *Flip the Switch* is to encourage you to actively choose the right behaviour in order to achieve more at work, at home and in your everyday life.

For this to happen in the corporate world, for instance, organizations must embrace the idea that corporate identity, mechanics and metrics don't make a company. Lip service towards valuing individuals within organizations only goes so far. We all possess the ability to flip the switch, but if we do not become more conscious of, and act on, this innate ability now, we are at risk of further narrowing the gap between stimulus and response – to detrimental effect.

The phenomenal and seemingly continual advances in technology have given rise to our ability to access information immediately and to respond to stimuli faster than ever before. Not only does technology allow us to have multiple conversations at any one time but it also allows us an insight, or snapshot of people's lives. In doing so, this encourages us to pass quicker judgement; offering us the ability to respond and react in an instant. All without considering the consequences of our behaviour. Cue flashback to emails you regret sending almost immediately after pressing "send" and the flippant remark you fire off on a friend's Facebook post, only to have to handle the backlash.

The result of some of the rapid technological advancement, especially in the field of communication, is a lack of behavioural consciousness, and it is endemic. Given how automatic and subconscious much of human behaviour is, it is perhaps unsurprising that we have adapted so well to the effects technology and societal changes are having on our behaviour. However, the fact is that most people are largely unaware of their behavioural choices; the actions they take are less considered and the assumption is that they are more "instinctive". That is to say that fewer of us take time to think before we act.

I have spent the past three and half years researching people who have achieved extraordinary things or led extraordinary lives. My intention was to discover if there was something that we could all learn, in order to exceed our own expectations of what we are each capable of. I was driven by the possibility that this could lead to an understanding of how we could all enhance the quality or quantity of our achievements; perhaps even to feel surprised and more fulfilled by our output. Was there a way in which these people were behaving that was different and that helped them to exceed expectation, which perhaps we could learn from in order to alter our own responses to stimuli? Very quickly a pattern emerged. They were all more aware of the gap between stimulus and response, which Dr. Frankl talked about, and their choices were generally more considered based on the conscious consequences of their actions.

The result is clear: if we can learn to widen the gap between a stimulus and our response, our behavioural response will be more conscious. As a result, we become more effective not only at responding to the stimulus but at influencing the consequences, too. Perhaps in turn we'll also take more responsibility for our actions.

So Why 'Flip the Switch'?

Is it possible to flip our behaviour; to actively choose an alternative one?

When you write a book called *Flip the Switch* it prompts people to ask a lot of questions. Principally: "what is it about?" and "what switch?" Which tuck neatly alongside: "why don't we see much of you anymore?", "is it about electrics?" and "you look tired". Fundamentally, *Flip the Switch* is about a set of simple yet powerful techniques and strategies to help consciously choose our behaviour. If we actively choose our behaviours we can in turn shape their consequences in order to get extraordinary results at work and at home. If you have ever wondered why we do the things we do and how to change them for the better, or have an ambition or goal and found yourself contemplating how to change your own behaviour (or those around you), in order to achieve more, you're in the right place.

My interest in people achieving extraordinary things and the very notion of normal, or ordinary, and extraordinary began in the most unlikely of places. It was a large stately home just outside Birmingham, England. The sort you'd see on a period television drama: deep oak panelled walls; flagstone floors; large fireplaces that were so big you could fit a table into and use as a novelty dining area; suits of armour nonchalantly displayed in corners – you know the sort. I had just spoken to a group of about 600 sales people about how to deliver extraordinary levels of customer service and the psychological effects it has on customers.

At one point, a person pointed at my moustache, smiled and said: "I love that!" I thanked them and they replied: "I think that's brilliant! Do many people stare at you?" A little taken aback at the notion of being positioned as something of a freak show by a complete stranger, I confirmed that it occasionally got an odd look from those reacting as if a curly moustache is the most remarkable or offensive thing they've ever seen. But otherwise, it draws more smiles and approving looks than the former. The person then went on to say: "Brilliant! And why not, hey? Normal is taken!"

Normal is taken.

Indeed it is. My mind began racing with questions to answer. Why would anyone want to be ordinary? Do people consciously know that they are ordinary? What *is* ordinary? Why be ordinary if you could be extraordinary? What is extraordinary? How do you *become* extraordinary?

Over the next four years, I started analysing the choices people were making and their responses to the consequences of their decisions; everyday interactions between people; people's responses to the situations they found themselves in; listening to and reviewing how they presented themselves, and spoke about themselves; their achievements and the justifications for their own behaviour and their critical reviews of how others behaved.

During my attempts to understand what extraordinary was, it quickly became obvious, to me at least, that if "normal was taken", there were significant commercial reasons that supported being extraordinary in business. If you are a teacher or lecturer, for example, it can have potentially life-changing implications for those you educate. The more I thought about the notion of not being like everyone else, of striving to be extraordinary in what you do by being more aware of your behaviour, I realized that there were important lessons for us all to consider. Over the past twelve years I have spoken to, trained and met hundreds of thousands of people. I've created hundreds of training videos, resources and development programmes in that time and in writing this book have used some of those resources, as well as stories and outcomes which have come about at seminars, conferences and communication with delegates, in addition to independent research.

This book aims to answer three fundamental questions:

• Why strive to exceed your own expectations, let alone widen the gap between stimulus and response? What's the point?

• What would the impact be on leadership, education, business and society if we made a more considered response to behavioural stimuli?

• How do we most effectively change our behaviour for the better in order to help us to achieve more?

It's a wonderful fact of life that every single day, ordinary people do extraordinary things: carrying out extraordinary acts and creating extraordinary results. Although, it's perhaps a more accurate statement that, in reality, some ordinary people sometimes do extraordinary things.

Extraordinary is of course subjective, and for the purposes of this book, without trying to be something for everyone, I'm sure you can recall an especially inspiring manager who you respected because of particular characteristics or attributes that made them stand out from others. Or perhaps a teacher who comes to mind as extraordinary in their patience and ability to encourage achievement, for example, or even an individual – a friend or colleague who always seems to handle things better, or cope with life's crises. You may well be reading this and thinking: "If you'd met my Uncle Barry you wouldn't be saying that." However, even those people you've given up all hope for are capable of performing at an extraordinary level and actively choosing the right behaviour.

Some people I've spoken to are too afraid to have a dream; feel silly about setting goals and don't have sufficient self-confidence to believe that an ambition would be achievable. This self-limiting behaviour, an active choice some people make, is the most significant barrier to achieving anything extraordinary.

Once, after I had presented to a group of researchers and medical scientists, I was asked to sign some copies of my book. Stood in the surprisingly modern space of the Royal College of Physicians in Euston, London, I asked a very intelligent and articulate research professor what she felt defined an extraordinary person. She said, with all seriousness: "I suppose a superhero or someone with super-human powers ... but then having said that, some of Michelangelo's works are quite extraordinary."

I went on to ask the professor how she would define extraordinary, and she replied: "I think something that is truly exceptional, far from the norm and out of the reach of most of us."

Now, this professor is a single parent who has been involved in some of the most ground-breaking research into cancer treatment, has had numerous articles and papers published in scientific publications, written best-selling books under a pseudonym, and who is humble only through a seeming ignorance of the impact of her very existence. I think it's fair to say that this professor is extraordinary. Yet she didn't consider herself to be.

The very existence of this book and the principles of *Flip the Switch* exist to prompt us to consider alternatives to what we believe, perceive or define as ordinary; to consider what we could do that we would define as extraordinary and to show how simple it is to actively choose and change our behaviours – to flip the switch.

The Value of Choosing Your Perspective

Each one of us is essentially made of the same stuff: we're all only human. Even if subjectivity rules and what is extraordinary to one person is merely normal to another, there's no denying that individuals like Mahatma Gandhi, Abraham Lincoln, Charlie Chaplin, Walt Disney, Mother Theresa and Martin Luther King were extraordinary people, doing something quite remarkable. Each have created lasting legacies and not only made a mark on the world but changed the course of lives for millions upon millions of people.

Many people argue that they themselves aren't the type of person that could be extraordinary or do extraordinary things. Or that it simply isn't possible to learn to be extraordinary – that it's a gift or ability that people are born with.

Even though our behaviour is a combination of nature and nurture, our ability to actively *choose* our behaviour based on the desired consequences or to do something that we consider extraordinary is learnt and nurtured. Thankfully, though, although parents, guardians and teachers have a lot of responsibility, we can nurture this ability ourselves.

For many, being extraordinary is a way of coping with the world. Perhaps a lonely childhood drives them to do things that make them stand out and in turn attract attention and gain popularity. Or being constantly told that they couldn't do something or weren't clever enough unintentionally empowered them to prove that they could indeed do things they had their heart set on.

I myself suffered with fairly regular transient bouts of depression through my mid-teens and well into my late 20s, which at the time I was relatively confident were all just part of growing up. Not that this understanding made it any easier. Those dark moments of loneliness, anxiety, sleeplessness and struggling to come to terms with the emotional pain I experienced were somewhat numbed and distracted by listening to music to get myself to sleep. However, it is these very experiences that cause so many people to drink or take drugs to escape the pain and that quickly develops into a very dangerous coping mechanism. I often wondered why I didn't turn to those things; what made me choose ants, trees and sunsets instead of cocaine and cheap cider? How was I able to flip the switch and choose a different response to those stimuli?

I grew up in the countryside, and where some find it fantastically lonely, I have always found it more than beautiful. Walking my dogs across fields was a welcome escape from reality and it still serves as great thinking and quiet time. I remember the first time I experienced my first real high in life. I was about 14 and shopping in the local town, stood by the clock tower, and as I looked down I noticed a few ants, speedily scurrying around. One of them was carrying a piece of a leaf and I'd read somewhere that an ant can carry an item up to twenty times its own body weight.

I don't know how long I watched those little ants but I do know that when I looked up and saw the people, the cars, the tall clock tower and the buildings around them, I was amazed. What an incredible world. These tiny creatures have absolutely no comprehension of us; no idea of how wonderful our world is: the intelligence, the construction, the progress and the history. And they don't need to, either.

I got on a bus home and couldn't stop thinking about the fantastic antithesis of our two worlds. I imagined a film where the camera was tightly focused on the ants that I was watching, scurrying around so quickly, their existence consumed by finding the path home and carrying their leafy dinner —and as it zoomed out you saw the scale of the ant compared to the paving slab it was on, compared to a human, compared to a car, compared to a building, still zooming out as you see a town, a county, an entire continent and finally Earth, floating in space. I've never forgotten that amazing, enlightening moment, which for me put life into perspective. How can you not be impressed by the wonderful world that we live in? It's just a shame that all too often humans make poor decisions and create some sensationally bad things that result in extraordinarily negative consequences. So, instead of preparing a vein, I became fascinated with what are essentially natural wonders and highs and, more importantly, how you can choose the way that you respond.

I've written this book to share with you some remarkable techniques that you can use at work, at home and in your everyday life. The very principles of flipping the behavioural switch help to make extraordinary things happen. By being conscious of our behaviour, we are able to make more informed choices, which result in more predictable consequences. Furthermore, it helps shape those consequences and highlights the importance of what I am concerned could become a real social issue of the future, which we can all avoid if we act now.

We must teach our children to become more conscious and selective of their behaviour; to prevent the immediacy of their responses so encouraged by technology. If we don't do something about it, I fear that we are in danger of killing our freedom. I've developed the resources over the years with my clients, audiences and those I coach to help you to exceed the expectations of what you believe you can achieve; to take whatever you currently do, or whoever you currently are, out of the restraints of ordinary and make the step-change to achieve something altogether extraordinary. These principles have worked for me – and continue to do so – and for the hundreds of thousands of people I have taught them to and I know they will for you, too.

I'm going to offer you the opportunity to flip the switch throughout the book: to pause and spend more time in the gap between stimulus and response and there's a very good reason for this. Research conducted originally by IBM and then repeatedly by the UK Post Office demonstrated that the ability to recall information, and therefore its ability to change our behaviour, dramatically declines when we are only told something. This chart shows why it is important to not just read this book but to interact with it for best effect:

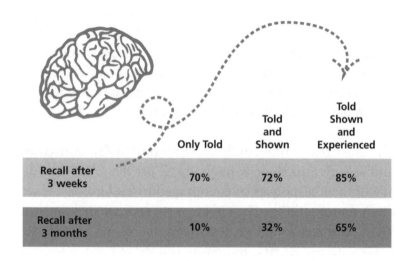

	Only Told	Told and Shown	Told Shown and Experienced
Recall after 3 weeks	70%	72%	85%
Recall after 3 months	10%	32%	65%

A common theme of the people I studied and interviewed, who had all achieved something extraordinary in their lives – and many who continue to do so – was that they think and are motivated in ways quite different to most people. The problem is that ordinary is more often than not more than acceptable: things get done; children learn and sales are made without anything more than ordinary experiences or inputs. All of these achievements and many more besides are perfectly possible on "behavioural auto-pilot".

We are incredibly resilient as a species and have a quite remarkable ability to bounce back. But those ordinary experiences are easily forgotten – nothing stands out about them. It's the extraordinary experiences and the extraordinary people that often make the biggest impact and differences – these are the people that stand out. And understandably so. Subsequently they are often the most successful, too. Why are the likes of Walt Disney, Nelson Mandela, Jane Goodall, Albert Einstein, Richard Branson, Sir Ken Robinson, and Mahatma Gandhi so well known, revered and praised? Why are their actions, thoughts, contributions and legacies so memorable and widely shared? Certainly not because they thought average thoughts, produced ordinary work and weren't conscious about the consequences of the behaviours they chose.

Ordinary is taken; it's time to be different; to flip the switch and actively, consciously choose our behaviour. It's time to start exceeding our expectations because we can. It's time to be extraordinary.

Jez Rose
Buckinghamshire, England. 2016
#BeExtraordinary

1

Find the Gap

....

"Happiness is a state of mind; it's just according to the way you look at things."

Walt Disney, animator, businessman, producer, director and loved the world over as the father of Mickey Mouse

Achieving More by Changing Your Mind

What is it that makes someone an extraordinary person?
Is it their abilities?

Or their talent? Or simply their smile? Sure, there may
be differences in the way they do things: the difference
between a winning runner and the one who comes second can sometimes be just a few kilojoules of energy,
for example, and those few kilojoules may well be the
result of a few hours extra training over the course of
many months. However, the key difference is their attitude, their mindset. Like everything in life, our perspective on things determines our response, our action or
inaction, and ultimately the consequences of those actions
and responses.

On the windowsill of my office sits a glass ornament with
Walt Disney's quotation about happiness engraved into
it. For someone who spends his life travelling the world
speaking to and training large groups of people, with lots
of performance elements to make learning engaging and
fun (the fallout of working as a comedy performer for
several years), I've ironically always been one of those

"no drama" kinds of people. If someone knocks over a glass and it breaks, or the dog chews a table leg, my first reaction is normally practical: did anyone die? (That's probably the result of having a background in medicine.)

My response is simply: does what happened affect anything immediately? Can we clear it up now? Much of life is not permanent, so if it's replaceable – well, it's replaceable. If no one died as a result of something happening, then the result can only be much better than the worst case scenario. That's the bench mark I use for nearly everything: did anyone die? Every moment you are living, somewhere in the world a family are gathered around a loved one, watching their life slowly ebb away; medical professionals are fighting to stem a bleed or otherwise save the life of someone as a result of injury; tears stream uncontrollably down the pained faces of family and friends at a funeral. It is sobering to put things into perspective because, quite often, we don't. We live our lives just in the moment. We become all consumed with ourselves and what we're doing right now. Our moods and sometimes our entire days are affected by the impact something has on us.

Of course, it doesn't make the things that do happen any less serious: a client is unhappy with what you produce, the cat is unwell or the car is badly damaged in the car park – these are far from positive things. However, we have a choice over how we respond to these. Crying, becoming irate and allowing yourself to be engulfed by stress are simply not going to make your client happy, cheer up the cat or fix your car.

Feeling despondent or running late? Left something at home? Shrunk your favourite jumper? Scratched the wooden floor? Missed your turning? Some people work themselves into a frenzy; their stress levels rise; they are in a foul mood for the entire day and spend the rest of it slamming things down and sighing a lot. As a result, those around you become irritated and in no time at all you have an oppressive and negative environment. This is all from one person who has allowed themselves to be affected by something out of their control. However, the one thing we can all control is our own responses. The most significant barrier to making the shift from ordinary to extraordinary, in whatever endeavour we wish to do so, is ourselves because no one else can do it for us.

Be Mindful of Who You Spend Your Time With

One thing that has a significant impact on our behaviour and on the decisions we make is who we spend time with – either by default or design.

Our behaviours, responses, characteristics and even language are all heavily influenced by who we spend time with, so it is especially important to populate our life with those who will make a positive difference to our lives as a result of being around them.

I am reminded by a fridge magnet with the old adage: "you can choose your friends but you can't choose your family". While you may not be able to choose your family, you can choose how much time you spend around them – and your friends – and what to talk about – to protect yourself from how they might make you feel.

Expanding the Gap between Stimulus and Response

We can all identify those moments in life when we have become so wrapped up in what is essentially something of little to no consequence in the grand scheme of things – a non-problem.

It is all around us in road rage, offices, queues, internet forums, customer service interactions, educational settings, childcare and at home; in all of these areas we experience people who appear to lose the ability to maintain rational thought. The smashed glass no longer matters – it is beyond repair; and so going forwards we should replace it or move on.

My Grandma used to say: "There's no point crying over spilt milk." Neither is there any point in crying over the selfish person who was in a rush and cut you up, or the arrogant shop salesperson. We do seem to have a strange predisposition as a species to not be especially realistic in our reasoning. I'm not surprised at the term "armchair philosopher" when I watch a reality television show with people making accusations and assumptions as the news broadcasts on their television, or having a twitch at the net curtains and revealing an opinion about where a person has been, where they are going or passing judgement on their life.

Many years ago when I was working in healthcare, I remember holding the hand of a dying man called Frank. He had terminal throat cancer and was especially kind natured and selflessly thoughtful; one of those people you meet and wish you'd known for longer. He was old by the time I met him; I can't remember exactly how old but late 70s, I imagine. Frank's wife held tightly onto one of his hands and I gently held the other. Frank looked at me with his glassy, steel-blue eyes and said in his slightly gruff voice, with a sombre hint that he knew exactly what was coming: "no one lives forever". Frank died just a week or so following that.

For the rest of my life I shall remember that moment and how it almost instantly put everything before, then and forevermore into perspective: the time I shouted and swore at a car that had cut me up; how upset and irritable I'd got when I smashed my own favourite mug; when I was running really late for a friend's wedding and ruined the rest of the day for myself because I was so stressed and angry.

For me, largely because of that moment with Frank, I appreciated that all of the things that had happened to me in life up until that moment had passed me by. They'd just happened to me. There were many really wonderful times, memorable achievements and the occasional sad time, too. However, I had my head down and was getting on with my life, seemingly like most of us. I see this everywhere I go – very little appreciation of the fragile and finite properties of life. We are here but once, yet the way people move around you would be forgiven for thinking that this was merely a rehearsal and that we will get to do it all over again, playing out those parts we didn't quite get right with a renewed vigour, flamboyance or tact that we failed on the first time around.

It was about the time that I met Frank that it occurred to me that not always doing what is considered normal, making an effort to reach for something more than what we expect ourselves to be able to achieve, was the key to many things: being successful in business, finding happiness, creating memorable moments for others, being better teachers, nurses, directors, parents – or indeed people. We can all perform at a greater level and create a more significant impact when we ask ourselves: "Why?" Fellow TED speaker, Sir Ken Robinson, challenges why schools teach in restrictive timetables, which force students to choose topics of study they may not necessarily like and don't make the most of their individual abilities. Why do we invite armchair philosophers, with no legal training, onto a jury to make unqualified opinions and decide the fate of others? Why do religions that support love cause so many wars? Why are you, you? We should question ourselves more: our thoughts, our behaviours, our beliefs.

I am certainly not suggesting that we question the status quo in order to go against the grain or be intentionally obstructive.

But if you do nothing, nothing will happen. It is the safest and easiest place to be but it is possibly also the least interesting, offering the least variety and stimulation. There is nothing extraordinary about ordinary.

So the first part of our journey towards flipping the switch begins with *you*. We simply cannot simultaneously keep one foot on where we are now and make a step towards where we want to be or what we want to do. Making that step is simply the start of the process. If people can rebuild their lives from the lowest point of homelessness, with not a single penny to their name, then you can easily correct something that goes wrong and choose a response based on your understanding of the consequences. In many ways it is simply a matter of mindset: those things that we believe we can do, we do – and those things we don't believe we can do, we don't.

Behaviour as a Legacy

The notion of how our behaviour can influence our ability to be extraordinary is one very close to my heart. As I write this I receive news that my Grandma, Gwendoline Pearl Cunliffe, who has dementia and was moved into a home about six months ago (a decision I was never supportive of, protesting my evidence that it was likely to make her worse – it did), probably doesn't have long left to live. She's not eating and is drinking very little; simply sitting in a chair, her life ebbing away. It is most likely that nearly every person reading this book will have experienced the tragic loss of a loved one and will be able to relate somewhat to my pain. However, my Grandma really was someone quite special. I know everyone says that, but she really was.

On her 60th birthday, she thought nothing of parachuting out of a plane; the enlarged photograph of her standing in a ploughed field in front of a crumpled parachute, beaming with that trademark twinkle in her eyes and rosy cheeks, was hung with pride on the wall by the stairs in her home. On a few occasions she had to stay in hospital;

for a new hip and after a fall – the usual when you're over 50.

However, something quite extraordinary happened on more than one occasion when she was hospitalized. She received thank you cards when she left – from the hospital staff. She literally lit up a room with her smile, twinkling eyes and laughter. She talked to anyone and everyone – much to the irritation of my Granddad. Beautiful in her youth and right through into her elderly years, she was of the generation who had really charming qualities that we seem to have lost today: she dressed impeccably whenever she went out and was wonderfully polite to anyone that would stop to chat with her. My Granddad used to have to sometimes literally drag her away! As the second grand-child of the family and within just a thirty-minute drive of my Grandparents' home, I was doted on, with baking, camp-building in the dining room – which involved moving the furniture and draping bed sheets and blankets over the chairs – playing at being a shopkeeper in the garden using the low wall as a counter and having access to a huge box of Lego. Grandma had a heart and spirit that many would say was saintly and an energy and youthful-ness that masked her true years. Grandma would not sit still, literally – she was always on the go, with the exception of eating, playing the piano or the odd "forty winks". She had no favourite chair as so many older people do.

As soon as she woke up she would be up and doing some-thing again: cleaning, baking, mending, gardening, wash-ing. In recent years she was given a walking frame to help her with her balance. Getting her to use it slowly and not push it around so quickly was a constant battle, her mind was always one step ahead of her body. She thought of it as getting in her way and slowing her down but watching her with it, and the speed she used to go, reminded me of that time my friend and I were at the dog race track and he got his shoelace stuck in the electric hare. Some things just take off.

I remember clearly the first couple of years of her dementia setting in – not that back then we thought it was anything more than a few transient moments of old-age forgetfulness. But, oh, we laughed about it! That wicked sense of humour, tear-inducing laughter and ability to find the positive in everything: "what's your name again?" would bring a good five minutes of fun such that our sides would hurt and we'd have to try our hardest not to inflict any more laughter pains! But the memory lapses and confusion gradually got worse and the first time I knew it was serious and had gone past the point of no return was when I went to visit her in their bungalow in Dereham in Norfolk. I walked into the front room to see her, sat in a chair (which is where you now always see her).

It was like a train had hit me right in the chest. I can't describe the instantaneous, hard realization that hit me. The sparkle in her eyes had gone. They were dull. She looked overweight, grey and spent much of my visit being nasty, rude and obstructive. I cried for most of the two and a half hour journey home. That visit and subsequent time spent thinking about her made me realize how important our minds are.

That sensational organ tucked away deep within our protective skull, which we give so little thought to, will create the difference between ordinary and extraordinary. After all, what do we have without our mind and without our decisions and choices? What is the point in having health and a body that works if you can't enjoy it, understand it or even comprehend it? Our character traits, the choices we make, our beliefs, desires, passions, our preferences, our foibles, our hopes and dreams, are all rooted in our mind. It's a sad reality that those things we cannot see, we tend to forget about, which is the very issue social lobbyists have about so-called invisible disabilities.

Dementia is a cruel and devastating illness that slowly strips away sufferers, causing torment and suffering to family, friends and those around them. And although she isn't physically dead and I don't think of her as such, my Grandma, the Grandma I knew and loved so dearly, has been gone for some time now. I haven't visited for a while. I'm not keeping track of the days but I know it has been longer than I would normally leave it: it's not enjoyable for me and she doesn't appear to remember much of who I am, which probably hurts more than anything else. The favourite grandchild, with so many happy memories that now seem to pale into insignificance because the person I shared them with and who created them for me appears to have turned their back on them – and me. Now of course I know that isn't for a second the real truth and she isn't consciously aware of what she's doing – much of the time she doesn't fully comprehend where she is or why she is there. The extraordinary woman I once knew has gone. And you will have to trust me when I tell you that the world is worse off without her.

But what was it that made my Grandma extraordinary? I have never heard of patients receiving thank you cards from hospital staff before. Her love of people and communicating with others is certainly something you don't see much of. Something which probably reads as a rather ordinary conversation is propelled into the extraordinary for the other person. It stands out because it's different – it's a moment in their life that, albeit for a short time in this example, lingers and has an impact, as it doesn't normally happen.

Do We Become What We Think?

Fear often plays a significant role in preventing us from behaving differently: fear of unknown consequences and fear of the responses we might receive, for example. However, this is really only because of how habitual we are as a species: it's normal. We are creatures of habit, which is why we generally read the same authors, take the same routes to work and go to watch the same type of films. When you understand that this resistance is normal, it is much easier to flip the switch and make conscious choices to change your behaviour.

How many days have you spent working away at your desk until late at night, neglecting your spouse, your pets or your children? How often have you sat watching television leaving family or friends uncalled? How many "just this one" moments have you had with food and drink that left you overweight and unhappy? Indeed we take for granted the very fact that we are alive.

Some people appear to grasp life and the opportunities it presents and indeed create their own opportunities. These people aren't abnormal, however; they are, in a sense, extraordinary because it isn't common, it isn't the norm for people to readily make the most of every day or work to a positive solution. It is common, however, for people to focus on a problem, spend time talking about, debating and concentrating on something that has gone wrong, all the time not looking to the future for a solution.

So what can we do about changing how we approach the challenges and barriers that we face to positively alter the consequences? There are three questions I consider extremely important to help flip the switch and instantly change our behaviour:

1. Ask: "Why Does it Have to be Done This Way?"

This question is not designed to encourage you to be obstructive or intentionally go against the grain. It's to help push yourself to find new ways of doing things; searching to improve and challenge the status quo. Quite often you find that the only reason things are done the way they are is because "they've always been done that way"; they've remained unquestioned because of the over-whelming power of habit. This answer, combined with a resistance to change, is crippling for productivity and will prevent any movement towards changing behaviour. How will anything extraordinary come about if you keep doing things the same way? By repeating the same actions the same way you'll only ever get the same result, so looking at things from a different point of view is the cornerstone of doing things differently.

2. Ask: "How Can We Make This Better?"

In this one question you follow up the previous question, which challenges why you do things the way you do, with the solution: How can we – or I – make this better? Striving to always improve what you are doing, to find a more efficacious way of doing things is the best kick-start to actually doing it. Many of us are gold-star procrastinators and put everything off until the time is right. Only the time never is. In my experience the right time never comes, but this arguably over-cautious approach is that of pretty much every ordinary person I've ever met.

3. Ask: "What Would Grandma Do?"

Now, obviously, you don't know my Grandma – and more's the pity. But you can ask the same question about anyone else that you respect for making sound judgements and good decisions, to help guide you. My Grandma is not perfect. But everything she does has humanity at its heart and a genuine desire to do the very best. That's a fantastic role model to have and offers me a different perspective on whatever I'm doing.

There's also a lot to be said for not accepting the ordinary, which is what makes the "why?" question so useful. By not accepting what has gone before, you open up your mind to many alternatives that were previously invisible to you. If, for whatever reason, there is in fact no way to improve what you have been doing or the way you have been doing it, you can still ask yourself how you could do it differently – there's almost always something that can be changed for the better ... I find that sometimes in life, all it takes is someone else to do something that puts you in a position where you find yourself asking: "why didn't I do that?" or "could I do that?" Those moments that make you pause just for a moment and force you to consider your chosen actions happen all too infrequently in the rat race most of us are caught up in.

The Behaviour You Get More of is the One that You Feed

There is an ancient parable attributed to the Cherokee Indians, which goes something like this, from memory: a young Cherokee man is hauled before the tribe's elders, who are concerned about his aggressive tendencies. One of the elders takes the young man to one side and tells him that his anger is in fact understandable, for all humans have within them two wolves. One wolf is generous, humble and has an open heart. The other is aggressive, arrogant and selfish. The wolves are in constant battle with one another because neither is powerful enough to destroy the other. So his aggressiveness is only natural. The young man turns to the elder and asks: "but which wolf will win?", to which the elder replies, "the one that you feed."

Much in our own lives is up to us: our future and life path is carved out as a result of the choices and decisions we make on a moment by moment basis. Do you want to get out of bed today? Do you want to eat a large, fattening burger? Will you donate some of your monthly pay to charity? Will you stop and think of ways in which you can do things differently? Will you continue to work late, narrowing the time you spend with your friends and family? Will you allow yourself to get angry and consumed by negative emotions, or stop and do something about the problems? Will you take the motorway home, or the scenic route? The decisions we make every day determine which wolf grows.

Changing our behaviour in order to get extraordinary results is not necessarily always easy but it is actually relatively simple. It just takes a little conscious effort at the time to make the right choices and widen the gap between stimulus and our response.

 NOW, FLIP THE SWITCH!

The Two Common Behaviour Barriers

There are commonly two things that hold us back and prevent us from changing how we behave:

1 *A lack of conscious exploration of the things that are causing us unhappiness, or a reduced sense of well-being.*

Ask yourself at least once every three months: "What happens in my job that makes me want to throw it all in and leave?" You can of course apply this same question to your personal life: your relationship or marriage, for example.

Use this question as a reminder to keep an eye on your behaviour and the things which impact your behaviour – and to do something about it.

2 *A lack of understanding as to why we are doing something, or why we are involved.*

Explain to yourself, or others, why the task needs to be done. With a greater understanding of the reasoning behind the task, you feel closer to it, can conceptualize the task more easily and take ownership of it.

For maximum effect, take the time to consider what the consequences will be: what will happen as a result of you doing this? Furthermore, what will happen if you don't do it?

2

Choose to be Extraordinary

....

"All men dream: but not equally. Those who dream by night in the dusty recesses of their minds wake in the day to find that it was vanity: but the dreamers of the day are dangerous men, for they may act their dream with open eyes, to make it possible."

T. E. Lawrence, prolific writer, celebrated
British Army officer and Lawrence of Arabia

Your Extraordinary Quickly Becomes Ordinary

In Sir Ken Robinson's excellent book *Finding Your Element*, he writes about the sheer amount of information that humans are producing. As a species we seem to be almost obsessed with creating and distributing new information. For example, in 2010 the CEO of Google, Eric Schmidt, estimated that every two days we are producing as much information as we did from the dawn of civilization up until 2003. Isn't that extraordinary? Thousands of years' worth of information every two days. Yet this mass production, this blizzard of data, is now ordinary for us. It's just what happens today in 2016: we design, create, write, upload, share and transfer information at will – sometimes somewhat obsessively. It's a sobering thought that our extraordinary actions or characteristics may well be quite ordinary in no time at all. The huge amount of information being created on a two-day basis is testament to just what we can all achieve and enjoy being a part of.

Social media has certainly encouraged many of us to share our inspirations and creativity with Instagram, our thoughts, our hopes and dreams on Facebook and our knowledge and opinions on Twitter and LinkedIn. Yet many of us don't have the courage to publicly produce or share the information we have within our minds. We don't like the idea that we might be wrong and that others will critically judge our thoughts or information, so we keep it to ourselves: we learn to either not respond in a way that is true to us, or to close the gap, allowing any unconsidered response to surface because it's easier to hide behind this than to feel exposed about being honest and true about what we think or feel. Just imagine how much more information our species would produce if we all contributed the thoughts or ideas we had without fear of being ridiculed or being told that we're wrong.

Contrary to the popular phrase, there may not in fact be a book in all of us, but that doesn't make our perspective any less relevant. Taking an idea that you believe in and having the confidence to develop it, try it or implement it is the core of not only creativity and resilience but of increasing our confidence to trust the specific behaviour that we choose. Some behaviours you adopt, some things you try, will not work but that doesn't make them any less relevant if at the time they seemed appropriate. Many may not like the ideas you have, or agree with them, but you should feel comfort knowing that if your bursts of creativity, ideas or information aren't well received by some, there will be plenty of people who will embrace them.

Having Faith in Our Vision

There's no real reason why being able to flip the switch in order to shape and determine our future should not be of great interest to you. When I stand in front of an audience of 3000, or even as few as 100 people, I often get goose bumps thinking that there could well be someone sat in that room who has the ability, or even just an idea, that could help positively shape their organization, or even society as a whole.

Despite these lofty aspirations, you do not need a grand vision or to have experienced a prophetic dream in order to achieve something extraordinary, or to shift your behaviour in order to do something that exceeds your own expectations. Neither do we have to wait until we stumble across something worthy of an international prize before we do something about it. Your idea could be a simple one but may well have a big impact on how you work, think or behave or on how others work, think or play, or indeed to their life.

The air ambulance network is an example of something that is essentially quite simple: loading a helicopter with a specially trained paramedic and doctor with some equipment and flying them to those in need of life saving, critical medical intervention. Since 1989 when London's Air Ambulance, one of the first helicopter emergency medical services, was established, it has developed over time from that simple initial idea, to one that now includes fast response cars for when the helicopter cannot fly and has pioneered replica services across the country. It was one of the first services to perform open heart surgery at the roadside, and in the twenty-five years it has been running, has helped save the lives of more than 30,000 people.

It is somewhat chilling to consider that whoever had that initial idea may not have shared it for fear of being ridiculed or because of the many challenges and barriers they would face, resulting in the death and disability of thousands more people. I have no doubt that there were many barriers that Dr Alistair Wilson and his colleagues on the initial lobbying team at London's Air Ambulance faced, which at times may have seemed unsurmountable: clinical governance issues, initial financing, commitment to long-term fundraising, development of specialist training, logistics, permission to land and local and national government approval being just some of them. However, the belief in a thing is often all one needs in order to flip the switch to make it happen.

When we are faced with people who do not share our vision – perhaps through our lack of being able to clearly define what we envisage, or because of bureaucratic red tape, or perhaps obstructions from opposing parties – we can experience a strong sense of discouragement and disheartenment. It can leave you feeling deflated and far from motivated to continue. Whenever you experience moments like this, you should take comfort in the thousands of examples all around us of successful people. Success rarely comes easily. In fact, Thomas Edison is a perfect example of that. Not only did he rebuff the notion that he had failed to find a solution for his commercial incandescent lamp, as suggested by a reporter, but he publicly acknowledged that he had attempted thousands of times to find a solution. However, rather than viewing those attempts as failures, he positioned them as evidence that those particular methods didn't work, thus moving him on to the next idea. Eventually of course he triumphed. Comedians and performers on television are often referred to as an "overnight success" when their premier television performance goes especially well. However, what many do not see are the ten, fifteen or more years of hard work that has gone into writing, developing and crafting a performance that is good enough to receive widespread public acclaim. We don't see the countless performances in dingy clubs and pubs and far less glamorous venues; nor do we see the many times in which they failed to win much more than a polite clap from the audience, let alone a rapturous applause. In reality they are far from an overnight success. I remember seeing a poster in the office of a small business once; it said: "Sometimes having your own business is difficult – and sometimes it isn't."

When you temporarily lose sight of the end goal or no longer have a clear direction in your mind of that inspiration and motivation that first spurred you to change or start a project, you turn your attention to other things, or become frustrated at the long list of items on your to-do list that are still there, taunting you with their unchecked boxes and lack of completion.

Some days we just don't have the get up and go we had yesterday or the day before and some days, as much as you want to be focused, you just aren't. Yet other days you are on top of your game – and that's perfectly normal and expected behaviour for all of us; the result of myriad influences from insufficient sleep, digestion, alcohol, stress, overactive mental stimulation – the list goes on. However, this is exactly why the flip the switch concept is so powerful: the understanding that when faced with a lack of focus or a non-productive or negative mindset, we can readily change and actively choose how we want or need to respond in order to manipulate the consequences in our favour. So don't dwell on the things that you don't want; on the mood or language or situation that's holding you back. Instead, use that moment of conscious awareness to consider how else you could respond in order to realize a more beneficial short-term positive emotional outcome and long-term overall consequence.

⚠ NOW, FLIP THE SWITCH!

Start – Stop – Continue

Getting clear about what we need to do in order to change can be an enormous help in making the step-change needed to be able to easily, confidently and smoothly change our behaviour. This is an exercise I often use with clients either individually or in larger groups, which helps to focus on the specific skills, tasks and behaviours that are going to help or hinder your ability to flip the switch.

1 Grab a piece of paper now and write down the word "start".

2 List all of the things that you need to start doing: the things that you don't currently do, which, if you started, would help you be able to better manage your behaviour, offer up the ability to find the gap between stimulus and response, or consciously choose a different behaviour.

3 You might list things like focusing on the positive things that happen, pausing before responding to consider the best action, spending more time

---

considering consequences of behaviour, being more conscious of goals, for example.

4 Next, write the word "stop" and reflect on what hinders you: what are you aware of that you need to stop doing? Things like procrastination and responding quickly without considering the consequence might appear on your list.

5 Finally, underneath the heading "continue", consider which strategies currently work. What do you do that you need to continue doing because it works? Perhaps you are especially patient, are good at considering alternative actions, or have clearly defined goals, for example.

When Kindness is Offensive

When you first meet Robert Williams, you wonder if he's an assistant or a roadie to a rock band. He looks ordinary; the sort of person you'd pass on the street and completely forget about if asked to retrace your steps. I realize that sounds almost, well, offensive; however, you just can't help but expect the founder of The Kindness Offensive to look nothing short of extraordinary. It just goes to show how appearances can be so deceptive. I met Robert when he created what can only be described as a completely unexpected, emotionally engaging, soul-shaking spectacle at TEDx MiltonKeynes, where his colleague, David Goodfellow, spoke after me.

As David described to the audience what The Kindness Offensive did, Robert sounded an airhorn. Indoors. It was loud. Very loud. And into the auditorium piled some fifty or more people sporting smiles, hard hats, fluorescent yellow waistcoats and blowing party whistles. That was pretty surprising but it had nothing on what they were about to do: they began handing out shiny, wrapped packages as fast as their hands would allow. People in the audience were tearing open these free gifts and finding kettles, blenders, vacuum cleaners ... even a television! Brand new, unopened and absolutely free.

We had to do nothing; simply sit back and enjoy being thoroughly spoilt. And then – as David attempted to continue presenting to an audience full of giggling, over-excited adults transported back to a Christmas when they were 5 or 6 – explosions of confetti and glitter rained over the audience. As a behaviourist, I couldn't help but sit and watch in complete amazement – and admittedly, puzzlement – at the reaction this team of people were eliciting from us. It was a truly magical experience and the constant reiteration from David that these gifts were free and ours to keep and that they didn't want anything in return forced a lot of soul searching for a lot of people. This is the epitome of true kindness.

However, this wasn't a one-off finale. This is what Robert and his team do all year round. They are responsible for having given away almost six million pounds worth of items to date and for making a lot of people, all over the world, very happy indeed. They've featured in national newspapers, with full page spreads in the *Sun*, the *Indian Times*, the *Big Issue* and the *Independent* and have featured on the BBC, ITN, FOX and in many more international media outlets. None of the 6000-strong worldwide team are paid, giving up their time freely to spread the message of kindness and happiness. But why? And how on earth do they manage to get all of these products? It's not sponsorship; it's not by association and it's not endorsement. So how do you go about getting free televisions, buildings (yes, buildings) or top-of-the-range running machines to give away?

Ask – And You Will (Eventually) Get

Robert is one of the most genuine, reflective people I have had the pleasure of meeting. He's calm, honest and has a strikingly straightforward and sincere approach to his outlook on life. He tells me that it all started a few years ago when he was struggling to make ends meet.

As a freelance writer and musician, it was a series of unfortunate, yet expensive, events that led him to discover that you can get things for free, if only you ask. He didn't have the money to get a particular piece of hardware he required to fix his broken computer, and then found himself way off from the amount needed to replace his car's broken carburetor. And then there was the time he was hungry: he had nothing to eat and no money to get food with. What did Robert do? Did he panic? Did he steal? Did he plunge into a world of desperation?

"I called people and told them the truth – I didn't want to lie to them and while some people didn't want to help me, after a few telephone calls I soon discovered people were confused by what I was saying. They were surprised that I was so candid and just asking for their help. So they helped me and sent me what I needed, for free."

Robert soon ended up with a surplus of things that he gave to friends, including David Goodfellow who became especially interested in the notion that receiving free things and then giving them away brought happiness to them and to the recipients. David pondered, over free pizza, whether this process could become a thing to do, for other people. A job, of sorts. Could Robert and David become the real-life, modern-day version of Robin Hood? It's a humble idea and seems worlds apart from bankers and their big bonuses and corrupt board members and politicians fiddling expenses.

When I pressed David on why it was that they gave it any serious thought and what personal journey or analysis he had undertaken in order to arrive at the decision to dedicate so much time, effort and resources to this, his reply was enlightening: "Being nice and kind and altruistic are all good things to do, so naturally Robert and I were keen to do anything like that, but it raised further questions, which were interesting to consider, such as: Is being kind a good idea? Or is it just something that sounds good? We wanted to challenge those questions and set ourselves some targets that tested the argument but at the same time fulfilled the purpose: Can we get enough food to fill the soup kitchen? Can we get a company to give us enough toys to enable us to give one to every child in the local hospital? So initially those things were good for us but good for other people at the same time."

This notion of receiving goods and then giving them away became very much a twofold process; firstly to decide on a project that would make them feel good and would benefit others, and then to test it to see if it was indeed possible. As Robert quite rightly states: "We start with absolutely nothing and the result, the impact, is huge." I put it to Robert that what they are doing is extraordinary on so many levels, but his typically casual response was straightforward and simple: "We dare to try; that's all. Where other people think things can't be done or will be too much effort, they give up – they don't even try."

Determination Helps Achieve the Extraordinary

It would be easy to mistakenly think that The Kindness Offensive are on a moral crusade to change or challenge our way of thinking, but David disagrees: "We're not in the business of changing anyone's mind. If you make enough calls, you'll find someone with a similar moral compass to yourself and they will be willing to help you out – sometimes we'll set out to get something and if the mood is that this is going to be tough and might take some time, that invariably is the result: it takes longer than expected to achieve and we all find it hard work. Conversely, if we need to see urgent results or we want to get some things urgently, we'll end up getting them much sooner." If that's not a perfect, socially beneficial example of the effect of determination and focus, I don't know what is. Their greatest successes tend to happen when the team of volunteers work as a group, because when there are multiple telephone whisperers – the title given to the volunteers on the telephones doing the calling to suppliers – the group dynamic changes. It seems to create a sense of camaraderie and a reminder of the common goal, which motivates everyone to continue.

Interestingly and surprisingly, it's not all been plain sailing for The Kindness Offensive. They have discovered that some members of society and groups push back, resisting their great work. Likely through cynicism that something couldn't ever really be that good without an evil agenda.

David shares with me some of the criticisms they've had, which range from "you're not a charity" and "you're not a formal organization", to "you're commercializing the concept of kindness and encouraging children to want at Christmas …". The team have also experienced plenty of people offering advice on what they should do and how they should do it, but as Robert shrewdly points out: "The majority of people telling us what we should do and how to do it, when asked, hadn't actually exceeded at anything themselves. We had done so much compared to their so little and largely because we do it – we don't just think about it or talk about it; we dare to try it."

The impact that The Kindness Offensive and their extraordinary way of thinking has had is extreme and goes much further than handing out free gifts to people. Their regular gift-giving ceremonies to hospital children's wards, charities and organizations mean that they could quite literally make or break Christmas for thousands, and it's not an exaggeration to say that some wouldn't be alive today – having perished from starvation, of the cold or without having the luxury of a "plan B". That's an extremely important, poignant and heavy responsibility that lies at their door. It's one thing getting free pizza delivered, or being able to fix your car because of the generosity of a local mechanic. But becoming responsible for others is a whole different moral game.

The impact it has had on those volunteering for The Kindness Offensive has been just as deep, however. I ask David how it has changed him and he pauses to reflect: "It made me ask myself how free am I? What possibilities exist to me personally? It has totally changed my mindset and I'm a different person as a result of thinking differently. For example, I feel freedom in creativity and thinking and in being able to do whatever I want to do by just daring to do things. I'm welcome in more boardrooms than I ever was before, girls like me more and I'm in a better place emotionally and psychologically, with more socially important knowledge than I had before." Robert, unsurprisingly if you ever meet him, says: "I've been thinking this way for as long as I can remember. I absolutely expected this to happen and while I'm fascinated by it, I'm not at all surprised because the reason a lot of things don't happen is because people don't bother to make them happen. There's actually a lot of kindness in the world."

What these two men started, and have continued to encourage, is extraordinary. But what next? David's answer is ambitious as much as it is ordinary for them: "everything". Their drive is to give everyone in the world free presents and to encourage governments and organizations to consider making happiness and kindness part of the curriculum. Robert especially wants to see ambassadors for kindness, to encourage others to do the same. In the meantime, it's business as usual; they'll keep doing what they do because there's still so much opportunity to do it. David is keen to further push the boundaries. He's especially interested in finding out if this process has a glass ceiling because: "as big as we've dared to dream, we've realized each of those dreams". You can hear more of what Rob and David had to say in their episode of my podcast series *The Extraordinary Podcast*.[1]

Only Seeing What We Want to See

Rob and David aren't doing anything especially complicated. Their team of volunteers could be said to be simply giving away items, or wearing silly clothes.

However, it is not so much the choices that we make but the repercussions and consequences of those choices that affect our lives and the lives of others so significantly. The Kindness Offensive sees the consequences of their actions in the smiling faces of terminally ill children at Christmas; in the stressed and busy commuters who pause to receive gifts on their way to meetings and in the reactions of strangers on the receiving end of random acts of kindness.

Our ability to flip the switch and choose a different behaviour gives us the option of a different outcome, which in turn takes you further on your journey to comprehending the notion that we are much more in control than we may perceive ourselves to be. Many of us believe that we have free will, whereas in actual fact we don't. Not all the time.

The thought of someone else controlling our actions or influencing the decisions we make does not sit well with many of us and the majority of us like to feel in control of

---

[1]Listen to the podcast on iTunes: bit.ly/tepodcast

our own lives, or at least believe that we are. If we really did have free will, as so many of us assume we have, advertising and sales pitches would have no affect.

So why is it that so many of us feel that our choices are so free and unlimited, yet we respond so quickly to stimulus, become so absorbed by the impact of emotion and do not readily flip the switch?

When your brain holds two competing ideas, thoughts, behaviours or beliefs, it creates conflict – this conflict is termed cognitive dissonance. One common way in which your brain deals with this is to change its attitude, beliefs or behaviours in order to bring one of those competing ideas into prominence.

This makes us feel as though we have made a decision freely, yet very often we are at the mercy of cognitive dissonance. For example, have you ever made a decision, only to realize on reflection that it perhaps was not the best decision to make? However, despite this, you still stick with the first decision anyway? That is cognitive dissonance. And it exists because what we think of as our free will, isn't truly free.

The winning decision is determined by our context and historical behaviour, and in fact the same thing can be said for all of our behavioural decisions: they are simply a product of our genetic and environmental history and the habits that we have developed because of these.

I heard some remarkable and concerning examples of this when I attended a speed awareness course once. There are three parts of the course I remember well, and one of them was when Barry, one of the instructors, showed a series of photographs of roads: a dual carriageway, a high street and a country road. Our task was simple – to answer his question: "What is the speed limit on this road?"

The answers that were offered by the other twenty five or so attendees were alarming – they ranged from "fifty" and "seventy-five" to "ninety miles per hour". Now these were not young, inexperienced drivers. The majority of my fellow pedal heavy drivers were lorry drivers, with a few taxi and delivery drivers sprinkled in there, too. These were, in effect, professional drivers who were, frankly, making up speed limits!

The maximum speed limit in the UK is seventy miles per hour. It always has been. It has never been more than that. Yet over the course of time, presumably by driving at these exaggerated speeds, they have normalized these numbers in their mind. The power of cognitive dissonance saw them adopt the entirely fabricated speed limits in their minds.

Challenging Choice Blindness

All of us fall victim to this choice blindness from time to time, which is exactly why we need to question our decisions more and fully understand the choices we make, supported by facts or the very best information available at the time. Take a moment to look around you though and you quickly realize that very many do not behave in this way: they take information at face value. They have read something on Facebook and they then continue to offer this information, entirely unchecked, to everyone who will listen. You read something in a magazine or newspaper and accept it as gospel, despite the lack of evidence or balanced information, and you then proceed to repeat what you have read as a given factual statement.

If we are to actively change our behaviour by becoming more aware of it to perhaps do something extraordinary, for example, we must challenge this blindness to choices available to us, which could assist us in forming more educated and useful opinions. This in turn could help us to live a life less ordinary and make a difference to our lives and those of the people we lead, teach, treat, help, serve or assist.

The fact is that as a species we normalize things very quickly: our environments, behaviours, circumstances. This ability is useful in many aspects of our lives; however, it can also lull us into a position where we stop questioning, stop challenging and stop seeking improvement. The process of stopping to think, halting the chase towards completing goals and achieving deadlines, is extremely important for our own well-being; it provides an opportunity for us to realize our own achievements and to pause; to take stock of what we have got used to. Behaviourists call this habituation: normalizing to your state or environment.

A friend of my Mum's has recently moved into a large property. In the extensive grounds of this house stands a horse chestnut tree, which her two sons thought was the best part of the whole move: their very own conker tree! I saw my Mum just yesterday and asked after her friend and the new house and she told me something, in passing, which I want to share with you: my Mum's friends' two boys love conkers. They love exploring; they love being outdoors and the idea of playing conkers for them was the best thing about their new house. Just a few months after having moved in, the two boys no longer play conkers. Her friend told my Mum that the novelty of the conker tree had worn off. The boys had habituated to the abundance of conkers and now that little bit of magic had dwindled. What physical objects, people or resources are you surrounded by or have free access to that you once longed for or worked hard to achieve? What elements of your life have you become habituated to?

Interviewing and researching individuals for this book who have achieved extraordinary things raised some fascinating commonalities. For example, many of the individuals who others deemed extraordinary or to have done extraordinary things, refused to accept situations as given. They either believed that something else could be done or that there was another way or that things would change in the future. They also appeared to question a lot, too. They asked "why?" or "how can we improve this?"; "how can we change this?" It is through questioning ourselves and other people – our beliefs, our thoughts, our behaviours – that we can not only better understand why we do the things we do and how to change them for the better, but also quite literally train our brain to think differently and enhance our ability to flip the switch. If we all took time to pause before we responded, even just for a second or two, to use that gap to question more, it is not only ourselves that would, in turn, become better people, but those around us, too.

NOW, FLIP THE SWITCH!

Successive Approximation

The behaviours you wish to see more of must be positively reinforced. Be patient though and reinforce any and all behaviours that are even a tiny bit in the direction towards the final behaviour you're looking for. Don't wait out to get the complete, perfect, finished product because often we need encouragement and recognition of our journey towards the end goal.

1 Write a list of the things that you find especially reinforcing, that would encourage you to do more of the task that came before them. It might be as simple as some time on your own to eat your lunch in peace, or it may be something physical like running.

2 From your list of reinforcers, mark the ones that are simple to provide, such as going for a run or eating a square of chocolate.

3 Use these reinforcers to reward yourself for your efforts, or each milestone you reach closer to the goals you set.

What We Think, We Become

Those who work for The Walt Disney Company will be aware of the analogy of "on stage" and "backstage"; terms used to define areas and the associated expected behaviours of employees, or Cast Members as they are known, whether they are in public view or not. This concept of literally flipping the switch and modelling your behaviour appropriately is not just about making sure the public only see happy, smiling faces and tidy, clean areas, and are protected from the sight of Mickey Mouse with his head off, smoking a cigarette and Cinderella kicking back, bemoaning management.

Disney have clearly defined public and non-public areas so that the public see and hear only what the company wants them to, helping to maintain the Disney experience. This is a classic example of our ability to very simply flip the switch when the reasoning behind the choice of behaviour is understood. Those in leadership and customer service roles especially will be able to recognize their own ability to do just this.

On What We Focus, We Achieve

When we put our minds to it, it really is quite remarkable what we can achieve. Take weight loss as an example. Dieting and weight loss are global fascinations. According to a poll by Mintel, in the UK alone it is estimated that one in four adults is actively dieting at any one time. The poll showed that up to thirteen million people are on a permanent diet and according to consumer market research group, NPD, approximately 22% of the population of the United States of America are actively dieting at any one time. If you pardon the pun, it is a big business, and like most of the things we wish to gain control of or change, we reach out for assistance or for someone to do the hard work for us. I suppose this is why diet pills, books, regimes, weight loss DVDs, clubs and other para-phernalia that prey on the hopeful are so lucrative. We want the easy route. However, when it comes to weight loss, in much the same way as combatting addiction, the real work happens inside your mind – not your body. Let me explain …

If you think you need to go on a diet we will assume that you are overweight, which, without wanting to make huge assumptions, is probably quite accurate otherwise you wouldn't want to lose weight. In turn, because you think you are fat, you are most probably unhappy with the way that you look. That's not an especially positive way of thinking.

This negative mindset is not momentary: whenever you look at yourself in the mirror, bathe or get dressed, you see yourself in a less than ideal way. It reinforces that feeling of not being happy with how you look. In turn, you feel despondent and lacking in self-confidence about things surrounding your weight: your appearance, your weight and the clothes you wear. You begin eating foods which are comforting and high in fats, sugars and carbohydrates, which don't help with your weight loss. You begin to go out less because of your lack of self-confidence about the way that you look and your levels of well-being and hap-piness plummet. A lack of exercise and eating comfort foods exacerbate your weight issue and the vicious cycle continues. You become more and more unhappy because the weight loss you so desire doesn't happen.

As a result your mood changes and you become sad, which, in turn, plunges your self-esteem further into a downward spiral and you start taking less care of your appearance. All of this begins in your mind. Compare this with a positive outlook and a much more effective way to achieve what you set out to do, whether that be weight loss, to be happier, to sell more, or simply to be more mindful:

1 **Set yourself an end target, or terminal behaviour**: in the weight loss example it would be a target weight. In conjunction you'll need to set a deadline date for your goal: to be a certain weight by a specific date. You write it down and place your target and your deadline in places where you will see it regularly: on the fridge, on your bedside table, on the bathroom mirror, in your car.

2 **Spend some time visualizing your goal**: in this case, the way you want to look, reflecting on how looking that way will make you feel and spend some time reflecting in turn on those feelings of satisfaction and happiness. Reflecting on what it is that you're looking to achieve is the equivalent of asking "how can we make this better?" but you get to play it out in your mind.

3 **Revisit and read your goal several times every day.**

4 **Allow yourself one day of failure each week**: after all, no one is perfect. It's worth pointing out here that your day of failure is to be "banked" in case you need it; don't feel that you have to use it! Knowing you've a day reserved that you can call upon when it all goes wrong helps to maintain your motivation to succeed.

5 **Focus on every positive step towards your goal**: in the example of weight loss, it would be focusing on the

healthier things that you eat and seeing each day as a milestone on your journey towards a fitter, healthier and happier self. If you imagine a spiral as a visual metaphor for both examples, one is distinctly an upwards spiral and the other a downwards one.

You can apply these steps to anything you want to achieve, or set out to do, or to get other people to do. This technique of setting a very specific goal, with a tangible deadline and supporting yourself on the journey to your determined goal, is very often central to making that step-change from ordinary to extraordinary.

You will need to change the way that you think about and respond to obstacles and opportunities and the way in which you apply your knowledge and experience. Think of all of the things you could achieve, the places you could visit and the things you could do if you aimed to set yourself really clear, measurable goals in this way.

 NOW, FLIP THE SWITCH!

Brain Drain

This activity is an extremely simple way to quite literally clear your mind.

1 Grab some paper, or a notebook. Write down every concern, worry, item you're trying to remember and thought in your mind. Keep going until everything that's on your mind is written on the page.

You'll likely feel especially relieved just from this first exercise.

2 What you've now got is a collection of everything that is of concern to you. From this you can form a clearer to-do list, putting things into priority order.

3 Address each item, one at a time, until you feel comfortable that you are clearer about what steps need to be actioned.

4 If you are particularly creative, you may find that doodles or drawing also help to clear your thoughts especially well.

3

The Power of
the Brain

....

"A child takes something apart, breaks it up in order to know it; to force its secret. The cruelty itself is motivated by something deeper – the wish to know the secret of things and life."

Erich Fromm, German social psychologist, psychoanalyst, sociologist, humanist and philosopher

Rewiring our Brain for Success

Our brains are absolutely astounding organs. Yet, despite this, we pump our bodies with alcohol, tobacco and drugs, which all have a detrimental effect. However, if we were to conduct a functional Magnetic Resonance Imaging (fMRI) scan of your brain right now, we would be able to see where the most activity in your brain was at any given moment. We'd be able to ask you questions, pose conundrums for you to consider and ask you to imagine things so that we could see which areas of your brain were activated by the different tasks.

Following that scan, if I were to ask you to start challenging things more often, by asking, for example: "why do we do it this way?" and to then follow that question up with another: "how can we make this better?", you would begin, very gradually, to change the way that you think. You'd begin to approach things differently. If, after a period of time, say three or six months, we repeated the fMRI scan and I asked you the same questions, we'd notice changes. Your brain would be functioning differently, purely as a result of how you approach things, as a direct result of the language you'd been using.

Remarkable isn't it? We have the power to literally rewire our brain's neural circuitry. In understanding this, even at a primitive level, we are better able to put into context just how capable we are of changing our behaviour and why it's important to do so.

Over the past twenty or so years, much has been learned about how we behave and it's posed some serious questions about human potential. For example, we now understand that our behaviour today is not concrete: who we are as a person, the things we stand for, believe in, the way that we behave and think is not permanent. This means that we could be somebody completely different in six months than who we are today.

It's both enlightening and encouraging to know that we can change something as significant as the way our brain behaves. Of course, many things play a role in this that both accentuate and prevent this potential, whether obstacles are genetic or environmental, for example. However, this is exactly why we should challenge things more often and ask why it is that a particular process or activity is conducted in a certain way. That question alone is useful ("why do we do it this way?") but becomes significantly more powerful when coupled with asking how the very thing you are challenging could be improved ("how can we improve it?").

These questions encourage us to find improvements and changes that project you further towards achieving the extraordinary; different to what you achieve right now. They create a mindset whereby you are approaching things differently, looking at things differently and responding to things differently, too. They are simple, yet they are a catalyst for change.

When people understand why it is they are doing something, there are greater levels of engagement and compliance, so ensuring that there is clear understanding is important. I was approached earlier in the year by one of my clients, an automotive manufacturing company, to help them understand why their sales team weren't selling any more cars, despite "trying everything". I watched as the manager of a car dealership gathered his staff together early one Monday morning and said: "Right team, this month I need you to sell twenty more cars, okay? That's twenty more cars than our usual monthly target – do you think you can do it? That's it! Great! Let's remain motivated and focused, okay?" Now, at the end of that month, it did not at all surprise me that those additional twenty cars were not sold because no one other than the manager had any concept or tangible understanding of exactly *why* they were being asked to sell them. I explained that people often need to understand why they are doing something in order to buy in to the task fully, which offers a greater level of understanding. With that normally comes a deeper sense of emotional intelligence and connection with the task, too.

Following my critique, he assembled the team together again the following month and his pep talk was slightly different: "Right team, this month I need you to sell twenty more cars, okay? That's twenty more cars than our usual monthly target because one of our key suppliers has increased their prices by almost forty percent. This means that the profit margin has dropped by forty percent, so the extra twenty cars will ensure that we keep on top of our profits. If we don't sell those extra cars, we won't be making as much money and, as a result, we'll need to start removing some of the staff benefits. If we don't sell the extra cars, we'll need to let some of you go – do you think you can do it? That's it! Great! Let's remain motivated and focused, okay?"

As a result, it was a much more productive meeting and everyone left with a clearer sense of what it was that they needed to do and why – and with a clear vested interest in changing their behaviour. In case you were wondering, they sold almost double what they needed to that month.

Have you ever noticed how some people always blame others for not carrying out what they were told to do, when the only information they had to go on was what they were given? It almost always isn't the other person's fault – it's ours. We failed to communicate in a way that they understood, or didn't provide an environment where they felt confident enough to question our instructions, or we failed to check their understanding or failed to monitor their output.

Finding the gap and widening it has a role in getting better at accepting one hundred percent responsibility for our actions and the consequences of those actions. We can flip the switch and almost immediately go from someone who chastises others and always finds criticism in their work or in the results of instructions that we have given them, to considering the role we play; whether our actions could have been different and considering alternative ways of acting that will in turn alter the behaviour of others.

NOW, FLIP THE SWITCH!

A Personal Review

Ask yourself:

1 What things have gone to plan for you today?

2 What have people done that was correct?

3 What *didn't* go wrong as a result of someone doing their job correctly, or perhaps even going out of their way to prevent the occurrence?

It's a tricky thing to consider, because many of these things will have been expected and perhaps even gone unnoticed.

Now consider your response. Did you praise the dog for lying calmly on its bed, instead of running around barking or chewing the table leg? Did you praise your child for watching television quietly and calmly, instead of drawing on the walls? Did you thank your partner for helping to tidy up? Did you thank your colleague for arriving on time and for delivering on her daily tasks?

We Are Our Brain

Our brains characterize us. A healthy body and positive intent are all but useless if we do not have the control or purpose of our brains. It is a truly extraordinary thing, the brain. It only weighs 3 pounds. That's less than a quarter of a stone. Just over 1 kilogram.

Despite being this size, the brain is in fact a massive collection of cells called neurons – about one hundred billion of them. One hundred billion things that make you work; that form your beliefs, passions, knowledge, opinions, ability to learn and your behaviour, all contained behind your face. One hundred billion neurons. That's fifteen times the total number of people on earth. Now that is extraordinary.

It gets even more incredible though. Each of those cells makes contact with ten thousand or so other brain cells via a specialized system of communication connections called synapses. There are about 60,000 miles of fibres, which make up the components that form our brains. All of that goes around with you everywhere you go. It continues working under water, upside down and while being spun around, 365 days a year; our brains are undeniably the most comprehensive, intelligent and highly portable computers known to man. With something quite so incredible at your disposal, I don't know why anyone would not strive to realize their full potential, even if just out of curiosity.

Change Your Behaviour: Grow Your Brain

The American research psychologist Mark Rosenzweig demonstrated through experiments with rats that stimulating the brain makes it grow in nearly every conceivable way. Acetycholine is a brain chemical essential for learning; it is like the diesel of learning and it is higher in rats trained on difficult spatial problems than in rats trained on problems that are much simpler. Rosenzweig discovered that animals that are raised in enriched environments with swings, ladders, objects to explore and companionship learn better than genetically identical animals in environments without active enrichment.

As Dr Norman Doidge writes in his outstanding book *The Brain That Changes Itself*: "Mental training or life in enriched environments increases brain weight by five percent in the cerebral cortex of animals and up to nine percent in areas that the training directly stimulates." The reason this weight gain happens is because of the increased blood flow to certain areas of the brain. Just as a bucket gets heavier the more water you put in. The increased blood flow is there to support the twenty-five percent more branches and size increase of the trained or stimulated neurons of those areas of the brain affected by the stimulation or enrichment. Doidge also reveals that postmortem examinations have shown that education "increases the number of branches among neurons". This is significant because an increased number of branches drives those neurons further apart, which in turn leads to an increase in the volume and density of the brain. While you are most unlikely to have an increased brain size at the top of your goals list when it comes to reasons to be extraordinary, it does help prove my point and qualify that there is method in my madness to the years of research into understanding what extraordinary is.

So, you see, in many cases we can be very different indeed. The more your brain is enriched and stimulated, the heavier it becomes, or in brain terms, the "bigger" it becomes. However, a larger brain does not necessarily make you a better person and nor does it automatically give you rights. I have met many a fantastically intelligent person who turned out to be a complete and utter arse.

In changing our behaviour instead, as a result of learning more about why we do what we do and the influence we have over our futures, I would argue that we become more intelligent. Therefore, the exercise of flipping the switch could well help us to grow our brains.

 NOW, FLIP THE SWITCH!

People and Places

There are things we can be aware of to help us succeed in choosing behaviours to better affect our actions and those of others, too:

- **Make physical changes to your environment**. If it looks the same, it will feel the same. Environment plays such a key role in influencing our behaviour and helping to drive behaviour change, yet we pay it very little attention.
  You don't have to redecorate and knock through into a new extension; simply changing the layout of the room, adding more objects, photos, certificates etc., or even plants, can all help to make your environment look and feel different. The result is an environment that supports the changes in your own behaviour and helps to prevent you reverting to your previous behaviours, which will have been somewhat linked to the environment before.

- **Choose to involve yourself with others instead of trying to work things out on your own**. Isolation affects performance. When we don't feel included, we quickly become apathetic and perform at less than our full capacity. If you find yourself locking down and withdrawing into yourself, get out and about; spend time with friends or colleagues, for example, to maintain that sense of inclusion.

- **Be wise about who you spend your time with**. If you find yourself in a situation where the behaviour of others is problematic (for example a grumpy colleague), rather than tiptoeing around them, aim to focus on the more ideal behaviour, normally the positive one, or the results that you're aiming for instead. This can be difficult to maintain when the negativity coming from the other person is persistent, but remember that, generally speaking, whichever emotion is most dominant, will be the one that is more readily accepted and adopted.

- **Share best practices and techniques with others**. Start a programme at work to share ideas on how you are each able to choose behaviours. You could meet regularly and learn from each other.

We are surrounded by examples of just how regularly we change or model our behaviours, adjusting to environments or other people's emotions, for example. Yet more often than not we are not even aware of it – and that is what I'm most concerned about; our lack of consciousness when it comes to our own behaviour.

Distracting Our Attention

Richard McDougall, a former World Open Champion for his exceptionally skillful close-up magic and Gold Star member of the Inner Magic Circle – the highest level of membership of the world famous 'The Magic Circle' – has one of the most intelligently creative minds of anyone I have ever met and is much in demand for his contributions.

In his spare time he is one of the magicians in the Breathe Magic project, an intensive therapy programme for children with hemiplegia (paralysis on one side of the body). Hemiplegia can develop before, during or soon after birth or indeed later in childhood as a result of another injury or illness. The presentation obviously varies from child to child, depending on the site and extent of the damage to the brain; however, inevitably there is a degree of weakness, stiffness and lack of control on the affected side of the body.

Traditional occupational therapy often requires repetitive practice in order to make improvements, which often makes it hard for children to remain motivated. Magic, however, is therapy by stealth: self-reinforcing, intriguing and presented by default as fun, captivating and of course – magical.

The Breathe Magic programme is a ten-day camp that comprises the tuition of magic tricks and other bimanual activities (for example, children prepare their own lunch, cut food, carry their own tray, hold a knife and fork etc.) and playing games that require two hands. The focus for those participating is not on therapy or on their disability but on what they can achieve and what they want to achieve.

Extraordinarily, this revolutionary project produces more substantial and sustained improvements in the children's function than traditional therapy methodologies, but there have also been other extraordinary results that no one expected.

Emily[1] is 8 years old and was diagnosed with complex regional pain syndrome. Until the day when Emily banged her elbow, she led a perfectly able life, free of any disability and she especially enjoyed writing, playing the violin and street dance.

Banging her elbow was painful and caused a minor injury, but after the injury healed, Emily's brain was still sending messages that she was in pain. The pain messages continued and worsened until she was unable to physically touch her arm; she could not let anyone near it, or have anything touch it including water or even clothing, without it causing her excruciating pain. Even using a lift would result in screaming agony because of the vibrations caused by the lift's mechanism.

However, it was worse than that for Emily: simply thinking about her elbow or even moving her hand just a tiny amount caused her pain and distress so intense that her agony caused her to cry. She stopped playing the violin

---

[1]To protect their identities, I have used fictional names for the children involved.

and could no longer write. Teachers accused her of acting up and she became withdrawn.

Until one day at the Breathe Magic project when one of the occupational therapists at the Evelina ward showed Emily a magic trick, which involved reaching behind her back. Despite her being unable to move one of her arms, once she'd seen the magic trick, in true childlike wonder, she wanted to learn it.

What she saw was this: the magician showed her an opaque cardboard box with a lid. Inside the box was a cube and on each face of the cube a different picture. With the magician's back turned, she was asked to think of one of the pictures on the cube, place the cube back into the box and replace the lid, placing the box into the awaiting hands of the magician, held out behind his back. The magician turned around and told Emily which picture she had chosen.

She wanted to learn the trick so much but the occupational therapists knew that it would be a jump too far, so they started by teaching Emily how to perform smaller magic tricks, which required smaller physical actions in order to gradually build up a fractional opening of the fingers on her affected arm.

After a few weeks of performing magic tricks, which had been focusing Emily's mind on other things whilst simultaneously building up muscle function and an increased range of movement, she performed that magic trick which had first impressed her so much, putting the arm that once caused her so much agony, usually held close to her body and largely disabled, behind her back in order to receive the box. Her pain had stopped. The pain messages being sent by her brain had been reset and within days she was back to writing and playing the violin. One little magic trick changed one little girl's entire life.

What a gift. A magician for over twenty years, Richard has come to realize that magic is not about fooling your audience's brain – but more about fooling your own brain. It's all about looking at things from a different point of view. It is this ability to flip the switch and discover alternative ways of working, to achieve things considered previously impossible, that has helped to change so many people's lives for the better. Our altruistic tendencies often mean that while we look to help others achieve, we often neglect ourselves.

Very few things are permanent in life, which affords us the option to be much freer in the behaviours we choose, given that the consequences will largely always be non-permanent. In order for us to flip the switch, we must change the way that we respond to what is asked of us; to identify more of the stimuli that we respond to, sometimes subconsciously – and consciously challenge this.

This is especially important when we consider that our behaviour is influenced subconsciously almost everywhere we turn: from blatant marketing to the subtle language used by others. We cannot expect to always be consciously aware of when our behaviour is being manipulated, but as you will see in the following examples, the influence is wide and varied.

The Phenomenon of a Man in Uniform

Psychologist Leonard Bickman tested the power authority has on us in perhaps one of the most well-known social psychology experiments. One of his research assistants stood in the street and asked passers-by to do things, such as pick up a piece of rubbish, give some money to a stranger or move away from a bus stop. The research assistant repeated the same experiments over and over, wearing either civilian clothes, a milkman's uniform or the uniform of a guard. The results of the experiment were clear: fourteen percent obeyed him dressed as a milkman, nineteen percent obeyed the assistant when he was dressed in his civilian clothes and thirty-eight percent obeyed him when he was dressed as a guard.

While the results may not be surprising – after all, most of us have been raised to respect those in a position of authority – there are other research studies that support this notion that our behaviour and opinions are influenced by how others appear. In their enlightening study, Leff, Nydegger and Buck (1970)[2] found that patients perceived nurses to be less caring when dressed casually. Perhaps somewhat ironically, Stillman and Resnick (1972)[3] found that there was actually no difference in the willingness

[2]Left, H.S., Nydegger, R.V. and Buck, M. (1970) Effect of nurses' mode of dress on behaviour of psychiatric patients differing in information-processing complexity. *Journal of Consulting and Clinical Psychology*, 34, 72–79. Accessed online: http://www.ljemail.org/reference/ReferencesPapers.aspx?ReferenceID=1147766.
[3]Stillman, S. and Resnick, H. (1972) Does counsellor attire matter? *Journal of Counselling Psychology*, 19, 4, 347–348. Accessed online: http://eric.ed.gov/?id=EJ061505.

of people to disclose information to counsellors based on how they were dressed. Naturally, I mean whether they were casually dressed or wearing something more professional. Clearly no one would feel comfortable readily sharing personal information with a counsellor who was dressed as a squirrel, or Elvis.

Being aware of things that subconsciously impact our behaviour is important when your intent is to be able to readily flip the switch of your own behaviour, because it is these subtleties that may well exacerbate resistance to change.

How Hormones Help And Hinder

The neuroscientist Paul Zak is director of the Center for Neuroeconomics Studies at Claremont Graduate University, California. When he was a teenager he was involved in a "pigeon drop" con.

A man exited the toilets at a service station and approached the young Zak, holding a pearl necklace, stating he had found it on the floor. Fortuitously the phone rang at that same moment; it was a gentleman enquiring if anyone had found a pearl necklace. He had apparently just bought the necklace for his wife as an anniversary gift and was willing to offer a $200 reward for its safe return. Zak, eager to do the right thing, was only too happy to help. He informed the person on the telephone that a gentleman had just found it on the floor in the toilet. "I'll be there in thirty minutes!" came the reply from the other end of the 'phone.

Just as everything seemed to be working out for the best, the man who had found the necklace said that he was late for a job interview and could not wait for the owner; he had to leave. He suggested giving the necklace to Zak to return to its owner and splitting the reward. Zak agreed. He would make $100 and get to bask in the reflected glory of the man who found the necklace. However, not having $100 on him for the man's share of the reward, Zak took the money from the till, as a temporary loan until the reward arrived. He handed the man his half of the reward in exchange for the necklace and the man drove off to his job interview.

However, the man who had lost the necklace did not show up. Zak called the police, who informed him that the pearl necklace was not in fact real and worth just a few dollars. Naturally embarrassed and deflated, Zak confessed to his employer and agreed to repay the money from his wages.

Today Paul Zak is a leading authority on the neurobiology of trust. Understandably, Zak is interested in discovering why cons like the pigeon drop work and believes it may be down to the hormone oxytocin. His studies have shown that oxytocin is responsible for making our acts of cooperation feel good. When you feel trusted, your brain releases oxytocin and that in turn causes you to reciprocate the trust.

When the young Zak was lured into the pigeon drop con, oxytocin was released in his brain as soon as the opportunity to help someone arose. He was helping the man who found the necklace to reunite it with its owner; he was helping the owner to get his lost wedding anniversary gift back and he would be rewarded in cash for his actions.

Oxytocin is key to building social relationships with other people; we have an innate predisposition to empathize with others and indeed trust them. While some people do appear to be overly trustworthy, or gullible, it is as a result of both their biological make-up and environmental factors.

Does this mean that we need to be more cautious when we find ourselves wanting to help others? I'm sure it could well help prevent us from being taken advantage of by those less trustworthy. However, stimulus comes in many forms. Being conscious of the gap between a stimulus and our response not only puts us in a beneficial position with regards to our behavioural consequences but, in the case of trusting others, could well help us to be more conscious of how we are being influenced and why.

Our Built-In Ability to Adapt and Change

It was not all that long ago that the general consensus in the scientific community was that whatever we learnt was effectively ingrained into our brains for the rest of our lives. Once it was learnt, it could not be unlearnt. The belief that the neural network was concrete made concepts of behaviour change difficult, understandably.

Thankfully science has moved on. The concept of plasticity is just one of the results of scientific development and advances in our understanding of why we do the things we do (although there is still some resistance to some of the ideas presented). Plasticity is presented as the brain's lifelong ability (and that is quite key), to reorganize itself based on new experiences. So at any given moment, we only think we know what we know. But what we really know is what we can recall and it is that recall which is determined by what we have learned and how we have learnt it.

Neuroplasticity is the term given to the concept that a brain can in fact change. In essence it is an understanding of the brain's ability to change its own structure and functions through thought and activity. It provides a scientific insight into the centuries' old mantra: "what we think, we become". For example, if certain areas of the brain fail for whatever reason, due to illness or injury, then other parts of the brain can sometimes take over. This advance developed from teams of scientists who observed that children were not always stuck with the mental abilities they are born with; that damaged brains can often reorganize themselves, having one part of the brain substitute for another part that has failed; and, incredibly, one of these scientists also discovered that learning, thinking and acting can turn our genes on or off, thereby shaping our brain's anatomy – and our own behaviour.

Professor Norman Doidge suggests that this could well be "one of the most extraordinary discoveries of the twentieth century". However, Doidge warns that it isn't necessarily all good news: "[plasticity] renders our brains not only more resourceful but also more vulnerable to outside influences". Neuroplasticity is the reason, should you need one, why you can (and should), flip the switch and change your mind. It offers an explanation and scientific permission to think differently and be, within reasonable realistic constraints, whatever we wish to be. The concept of neuroplasticity is regarded as the reason why scientists have been able to teach people who have been blind since birth to see, the deaf to hear and victims of debilitating strokes to recover.

The area that is perhaps most useful for our journey is not the remarkable stories of how the brain has helped people to overcome physical challenges and disabilities, but the use of plasticity as a concept to rewire the brain to assist us with obsessions, phobias, trauma and – at its most elementary – our outlook, opinion and mood. No matter where you are right now, or where your staff team are, psychologically in terms of mindset, morale or even specific behaviours, we absolutely can – and I believe must – change these.

No behaviour is permanent (think about how you've switched to various brands when shopping, chosen to take a different route to a familiar destination or even started a new hobby) and nor is any thought, opinion or emotion. Each morning when I wake up, I actively choose to be happy and I choose to be positive. Admittedly that isn't always easy, especially not when the dark knight of depression plays its hand. However, to allow ourselves to act in any way that we are not completely comfortable and one hundred percent happy with; that does not best reflect our morals and ethical values, for example, is an example of how outside influences can shape us to become something that is not necessarily representative of who we truly are. If nothing else, plasticity helps us to understand just how fragile the stability of our mind is, how easily it is both influenced and corrected, and just why it is possible to flip the switch.

 NOW, FLIP THE SWITCH!

Accentuating the Positive

Regularly reflect on the progress you make, for example at the end of every week. It's a simple yet effective way to help shape your behaviour to become more positive, enhance your sense of well-being, improve confidence and focus and efficiency.

- Once a week, take a couple of minutes to reflect on the last seven days.

- Note at least five positive things that happened.

- Keep a record of them by writing those milestones down and review them regularly.

All too often we reflect on only the negative things because of the physiological impact these have on us. The problem is that it can quickly appear that everything bad happens at once as all of the negative things start to get on top of us, affecting our behaviour. In reality, of course, that's rarely the case; it's simply that we've been emotionally and psychologically placed to manage our time and the other things that haven't gone according to plan, but there have also been plenty of good things to distract us and make us feel positive. In those moments when it appears "everything is going wrong", it's normally the case that we're tired or distracted or haven't taken the time to reflect on our achievements and positive things.

As a result, the negative things take centre-stage and it appears to our battle-weary mind that everything is going wrong. If you want to be a more positive or happier person, or have a more positive outlook on life, keep a mental tally of every single step closer you are to what you want to achieve. The negative things, the mistakes and moments drifting off course, don't get any free head space; they are sieved for anything worthy to add to the experience bank and then cast aside. The only things worth holding onto are milestones achieved and lessons learned from the things that didn't go to plan, which in turn become something positive, which all help to maintain a positive drive and flip the switch.

4

Our Quest for Happiness

....

"For of all sad words of tongue or pen, the saddest are these: it might have been."

John Greenleaf Whittier, influential American Quaker poet and ardent advocate of the abolition of slavery

Choosing a More Positive Frame of Mind

The reason that the subject of happiness and well-being features from time to time in this book – either as a product of doing extraordinary things, thinking extraordinarily, or as the product of being able to flip the switch and choose a more positive frame of mind – is two-fold.

Firstly, somewhat selfishly I admit, it is easier to type "happy" and for you to grasp what that means as an example of an appealing, positive emotional response and state. I will not attempt to define happy here, but can we agree that in the context of this book at least, it includes the feeling of contentedness, cheerfulness and enjoyment: is that okay?

However, the main reason for using the term "happy" is that happiness is the root, the main driver, for most of our actions, life decisions and dreams. How do we know this?

❗ NOW, FLIP THE SWITCH!

Really Understanding Why

This is a very simple exercise that you can do for yourself right now and indeed with others:

- Consider what your dream or ambition is, whether it be a personal or professional one. You might answer: "I want to move to a third world country and help prevent world hunger." You might respond: "I want to be rich." You might have multiple ambitions. However you answer, be clear.

- Whatever initial answer you give, ask yourself "why"?

- Now answer that challenge of "why"?

- For each new answer you give, again ask yourself "why"?

- You may begin to find it more complicated as the exercise pushes you, and anyone you ask, to think about what it is that is driving these desires, choices and behaviours you have or have the ambition to achieve.

- Eventually, in almost every case, you will likely reply to "why?" with: "to be happy".

Are We All Searching For Happiness?

I was talking about this very thing to a colleague of mine, Terry Gormley, recently. Terry, like me, coaches individuals and teams; however, where my clients are mostly from all areas of business, Terry works a lot with sportspeople. He was asked to speak with a team of rugby players in order to assist them with focus and their behaviour on the pitch. One of the players was especially rowdy and causing a few problems with shouting out and showing off in front of his fellow team mates. One thing you should always avoid when working with psychologists, behaviourists or good coaches is being a wally. Any behaviour that is not naturally your own, we can spot from the second we lay eyes on you.

So, naturally, Terry has singled out this one individual as being a bit of a wally. Terry asks him: "Why do you play rugby?" To which he flippantly answers: "For the money!" to the cheers and jeers of his team mates. Terry looked at him and said: "No you don't." This response caused an increase in the surging flow of testosterone in the rugby player, if there was indeed any more that could be generated. "Yes I do," came the reply. "You don't," said Terry, "you don't play rugby for the money, so why do you play it?" The rugby player, now glaring at Terry, responded again: "Yes. I. Do." Terry changed tack: "Okay, what do you do with the money you earn?" The player thought momentarily and replied with: "I buy nice things for my wife and daughter." "And by buying nice things for your wife and daughter, what does that do to them?" The player considered this, furrowing his eyebrows. "It makes them happy." "Exactly," said Terry, "you play rugby because it makes your wife and your daughter happy and in turn that makes you happy."

The quest for happiness is at the very core of most of our decisions and choices, all-be-it not necessarily consciously. Think about that because it is critically important to a better understanding not only of your own behaviour, but that of others, too. Why is it that you bought a new sofa? You may well answer with practical reasons: "The other one was old and I was fed up with the mice that had burrowed into it" or "we needed a new one". However, no matter what practical reasons you offer, at the very root is the fact that buying a new sofa would make you happier.

It may well be that you find happiness through greater comfort or the absence of the smell of mouse urine but, nonetheless, happiness is the driver. What about the reasons we end relationships? Again, you might offer practical reasons that are at the forefront of your mind: "I couldn't stand the way she left the toilet seat down, made the house stink of nail polish and obsessively played Backstreet Boys really loudly when cleaning." The differences in musical taste and bathroom habits may well have driven you apart, but by separating you will in turn find happiness through less intrusion into your own life preferences and habits – and you know that. You are well aware that these things are not making you happy and that by changing them you will realize happiness, but the consciousness of them lies in the gap between stimulus and response. Very often the reasons we provide to justify our behaviour to ourselves or indeed to others are not readily considered. Sometimes it is the simple things that can have the biggest impact. My Grandma used to say: "Smile a while and while you smile another will smile and soon there's miles and miles of smiles because you smiled."

! NOW, FLIP THE SWITCH!

A Little Time for You

1 Write a list of all of the things that you do currently, in random order of importance, which make you happy, or the components, which actively get you closer to where you want to be. (This is your "B", as identified in the A B Split Test that we look at in more detail in Chapter 6).

2 What are the qualities and skills that you most need in order to reach your goal? For example, you might list time management; clear goal setting; professional development in training; communication; walking the dogs; time out with friends; playing tennis; cuddling your son.

3 Now rate yourself on each of these from 1 to 10 based on how good you are at carrying them out, where 1 is appalling and 10 is perfect.

4 When you have finished rating yourself, draw a vertical line next to the numbers, or grab a different coloured pen.

5 For each thing listed, consider a realistic target rating to set yourself that you could reasonably hope to develop to. Perhaps by improving, it will help you to achieve your "B", or goal, quicker, and/or that will make you happier.

For example, if you listed "playing tennis" as one of the things that makes you happy, but rated yourself currently at 5 because you don't play as often as you'd like, you might put a target rating of 7, for example, that denotes that playing a bit more, but not double the amount more than you currently do, would certainly make you happier.

Another example might be if you listed time management as one of the things that you do that either helps you get to your goal, or perhaps even makes you happy, and you rate yourself at 7; you might know that by improving your time management skills and therefore putting a target rating of 9, you'd not only achieve your goals faster but also be happier.

This exercise is not just about the acute feeling of happiness, it helps you to bank more positive experiences, which reduces stress and enhances your level of wellbeing. In turn this helps you to feel more relaxed, enabling you to concentrate more and become more conscious of finding and widening the gap between stimulus and response. The result is a greater skill in being able to readily flip the switch.

Flip the Switch through Gritted Teeth

In 1989 Robert Zajonc, a social psychologist who would later become known for his work on social and cognitive processes, published one of the most significant studies ever conducted on the emotional effects of smiling. He had his participants repeat certain vowel sounds that stretched the facial muscles into a shape that mimicked that of a smile, for example they were asked to make long "e" sounds. The participants reported feeling happier after making the long "e" sound and not feeling as happy when making a long "u" sound, which forced the facial muscles into more of a pout. Zajonc took this a step further and showed some groups of participants images of facial expressions; another group were shown the images and asked to make them and yet another group were asked to make the facial expressions while looking in a mirror.

The resulting evidence suggested that smiling is a cause of happy feelings, as the participant's pre-study scores of their emotional state were overwhelmingly lower than they were following the experiment for those who used the mirror. This is because the facial muscles involved in smiling have a direct effect on certain brain activities associated with happiness. Since Zajonc's work, there have been a number of different studies and fluctuating renewed interest in the area of testing smiles and happiness. The take-home message is always the same: if you are having a bad day or you need to feel happier, begin by smiling because there appears to be a relationship between smiling and happiness – smiling causes happiness but happiness causes smiling. Admittedly, if you have lost your wallet and your mobile phone, it's unlikely that smiling alone is going to make you feel any better about it, let alone happy. However, it may well help you to actively choose more positive responses, because swearing and allowing yourself to become stressed won't get your possessions back but smiling might well help you to not feel quite so bad about it.

When I'm presenting on customer service and the strategies and considerations for using behaviour to elevate the level of service to something extraordinary, I often refer to how customers have an imaginary sign around their neck, which, if it wasn't imaginary and one could see it, would say 'Make Me Feel Special', because that is ultimately what every customer is looking for. Who wouldn't choose to shop somewhere that made them feel special, over another business that offered the same product or service? However, it is not just customers who wear this imaginary sign. We all do. Children have it and teachers need to know that. Your spouse has it and you need to know that. Patients have it; prospects have it – we all wear the sign that asks for us to be made to feel special because, at various levels, it is an innate human desire.

If you can strive to achieve making someone feel special, it is highly likely, by default, that you will have connected at an emotional level with that individual and, in the case of a customer, gone a long way to securing repeat custom and a long-term relationship with them. In the case of a teacher and a student, you will have instantly built trust and cemented a stronger channel of communication. It is because of an understanding of our innate human desire to feel valued, respected and wanted that so many stories exist from people raving about great customer service, or a fantastic restaurant your friend went to, or the way you were treated in hospital, or a product someone bought, or a favourite teacher at school – because these are recollections of interactions with people and experiences that made those people feel special in some way. They stood out as positive examples for the people involved and, as a result, they get recounted.

It is, I think, quite charming that many of our actions can have the side effect of creating happiness for others. I believe that happiness is a side effect of many things we do in life; however, it's very seldom used as a primary objective. You don't all that often hear someone say: "we'll do this to make our customers happy" or "let's do this; it'll really make someone happy". While that isn't necessarily a bad thing, I do think that being more consciously aware of the impact of our actions is critical to our greater success in life. After all, if sending a handwritten thank you card can help turn a customer into a loyal fan of your organization, and randomly sending someone a bunch of flowers to thank them for their efforts can make someone's day, should we perhaps not be considering the impact we can have on more people, more often? If we acknowledge that we can have such an impact on other people – and ourselves – shouldn't we be doing something more about it? What can you choose to do to help make someone else happier? What can you choose to do to make you happier?

⚠ NOW, FLIP THE SWITCH!

A Little Bit More of What Makes You Happy

It's quite simple to calculate if you would benefit from more happiness and well-being in your life, and how:

1 List all of the things that make you happy, motivate you or inspire you. For example you might list holidays, architecture, seeing friends, theatre or reading the newspaper on a Sunday.

2 When you've exhausted the list, score each thing from 1 to 10, where 1 represents the shortest time and 10 represents all of the time, relating to how often and for how long you do those things that make you happy, or motivate you, or inspire you.

3 The behaviour fix is simple: schedule time to do those things that are lower down the scale. We experience less stress and a greater sense of well-being when we are doing those things which make us happier.

5

Why We Do What We Do

....

"We admire elephants in part because they demonstrate what we consider the finest human traits: empathy, self-awareness, and social intelligence. But the way we treat them puts on display the very worst of human behaviour."

Graydon Carter

The Biological Threats to Following Your Purpose

If you're interested in exceeding your own expectations of yourself, by all means follow the crowd and do as others do; your ability to flip the switch is not contingent on being a leader, overly independent or even confident. However, you should remain aware of why you're following the crowd and your reason for being there. Follow with purpose. Although having a strong sense of purpose can very much be decided upon – a conscious thought and effort that we pursue – there are more subtle, biological factors that can also influence our behaviour, in the form of oxytocin.

Yes, the very same oxytocin that was involved in Zak's pigeon drop con in Chapter 3. It's a neuropeptide (which essentially means that it looks a particular way and it acts as a neurotransmitter, so has an impact on the brain) that is sometimes referred to as "the cuddle hormone" or "the moral molecule". I know, science sometimes doesn't help itself, does it? Produced in the hypothalamus, which is the slightly hidden bit of the brain that looks a little like a tooth, it is then stored and secreted by the pituitary gland.[1]

It is most commonly discussed in relation to new mothers because during childbirth and breastfeeding there is a surge of oxytocin in the mother's body that helps the mother develop a greater "mothering instinct": literally to decide whether to care for her child when it develops a snotty nose, for example, or throw it away. That's commonly where our understanding of oxytocin comes from. However, scientists went on to discover that oxytocin plays a role in all sorts of occasions of happiness; from helping us to recognize faces at a party and attribute the correct emotion to that face (think recognizing a good friend versus recognizing an ex who turned out to be the anti-Christ), to achieving orgasm. (Possibly with someone you met at the same party – I don't know your morals but if you only just met them and you're skipping to third base already? Come on now.)

The Effect of Group Mentality

Now, for me and many others in the behaviour and psychology fields, oxytocin actually plays a much more interesting role than simply the fluffy, popular portrayal of being a bonding hormone. Certainly, as Zak has demonstrated, it can have a direct impact on how we respond when someone asks for our help because of the role it

---

[1]For the biology nuts reading this, you'll remember it's specifically the one at the back, the posterior pituitary gland.

plays in whether we trust people or not. It has also been shown to influence whether we go along with the decisions of a group or not, actually acting to enhance our conformity.

While all this talk of oxytocin may have you wanting to reach for the internet and find out how you can have it pumped around your office and bottling it for those plug-in diffusers, you might want to bear with me just a few sentences longer because several experiments have suggested that while oxytocin makes us more generous and trusting, it doesn't actually make us any more gullible. For example, if you have evidence that you are being lied to or if something doesn't quite sit right with you, no matter how much oxytocin is flooding your brain you will still be able to withdraw trust. That's partly how the pigeon drop con gets the "con" part of its name: it relies on the acting ability of the con artist to successfully pull it off. Thankfully this means that we are all still consciously able to terminate a relationship or remove our involvement from a situation if we feel our best interests aren't at heart. While this might be reassuring, the final twist in the oxytocin tale is that while we can control its effects on our behaviour, if there is conflicting information to how we feel as a result of it, we really can get quite carried away by its effects to the contrary.

Humans are social creatures and largely we enjoy being a part of a group; that's one of the many reasons why team activities work so well in the workplace. However, considering all of the research, it suggests that we like being a part of a group so much that we'd actually be willing to hurt others in order to stay in that group and continue enjoying that feeling of collaboration. The desire to belong is commonly considered to compromise our ethical and empathic instincts. In other words, if we let ourselves get carried away, we could well end up in an environment that prevents us from being virtuous. We really do need to be consciously aware of our behaviour, rather than simply allowing ourselves to follow the crowd.

 NOW, FLIP THE SWITCH!

Being a Category of One

Remember that flipping the switch is all about being aware; coming off auto-pilot and being conscious of our behaviour. It's easy to get caught up in the moment and adopt the most common behaviour that's displayed. Here's two easy ways to come off of auto-pilot:

1 Counting to ten when asked for a response. It sounds too simple to be true, but this will buy you time to find the gap and consider the best response.

2 Practise saying "no" more day to day. One of the common reasons people offer for not following their own purpose, is that they didn't have the confidence to say "no". Don't be afraid to respond in a way that is more true to how you really feel – you can of course be tactful in your response so as not to outright offend!

The Poignancy of Passion: Discovering Fuel for Your Purpose

Without that desire to change what you do or the way in which you do it, there is no catalyst for that change. One of the most essential components of willing behaviour change is passion. There must exist a passion within the individual for change. Without passion, we lack interest, commitment and motivation. The fuel for that passion can be entirely elusive and it is sometimes the role of the teacher, or leader or friend to help discover the source of that fuel.

I remember when I was younger I became fascinated with magic tricks, an obsession that was nurtured by my family. It wasn't necessarily the methods of the tricks themselves which were of interest to me; it was peoples' reactions to the performances and discovering the techniques used, which have their methodology deeply rooted in psychology, which fascinated me the most. When I was very young I would stay with my Father's parents, or Nan and Grampy as they were known to me. My Grampy would occasionally take me for a drive in his car and, mumbling some magic words, would produce a real fairground around the very next corner. If it wasn't fairgrounds it was Easter eggs in the fir trees in their garden and, if there was a lack of local activities for him to take the credit for conjuring up, a coin would be plucked from behind my ear.

Fast forward ten years or so and I would happily get up early for school, come home and spend hours reading magic books way into the early hours of the morning. The early alarm to get up for another day at school didn't seem to faze me in any way. It was the same for some of my friends at school who were musicians and would be out until the early hours of the morning practising their guitars or playing in bands. With passion comes an endless energy, enthusiasm and motivation to spend most of your waking hours immersed in it.

Don't Take the Positive for Granted

We often find ourselves impassioned by the actions of others who interest, inspire or impress us, which in turn motivates us to do something similar ourselves. Only, when we begin, we frequently compare our Chapter One with someone else's Chapter Twenty-Five, which is not only fantastically frustrating but demoralizing, too. We're guilty, too, of not reinforcing the things we want to see more of in ourselves and in others. We're very quick to punish the things we want to see less of: children drawing on walls, dogs urinating on carpets, colleagues missing deadlines. We're not necessarily any good at punishment but we all like to think we are and are very prompt in handing it out – again, without much consideration of the consequences of our behaviour.

However, the element that has the biggest impact on our behaviour and that of others is reinforcement. It's a sad fact then that we're largely very poor at immediate marking and reinforcing of the behaviours we want to see more of. When people hand in their work on time, or choose paper instead of walls, or the dog chooses grass instead of carpet, we often take it for granted that things are happening as we envisaged, offering little to no feedback. This in itself is evidence of our lack of consciousness when it comes to choosing and encouraging the right behaviours and being more present in how our behaviour directly affects consequences.

 NOW, FLIP THE SWITCH!

Spot the Positive!

For the purpose of this activity, something positive is anything that is not negative. That includes things which are expected or even neutral in that they are neither overwhelmingly positive, nor negative. For example, your daughter putting some of her things away is positive. The dog lying calmly on the floor is positive. The absence of a derogatory comment from your boss is positive.

Those things that we actively look for, we naturally become hypersensitive to. Think about when you buy a new car and you suddenly become consciously aware of more of them on the roads. Set yourself a challenge to see how many positive things that others do that you can spot in one week. You might want to start with just one day and keep a written record or mental note of every time somebody holds the door open for you, fulfils a promise or gives way to you at a junction.

I'm always astounded at just how many positive activities surround us that we often completely neglect to acknowledge. It's a great exercise to not only restore your faith in humanity but to get a better gauge of the

sorts of things that we focus on, positive or negative –
think of it as a sort of litmus test for your ability to spot
positive behaviours.

It is critical that we let others know when they do the
right things and reinforce the behaviours we want to see
more of. For example, why do so many people enjoy giving gifts? The act of buying, wrapping and giving gifts is
reinforced by the delight of the recipient and the feeling of
reflected pleasure. Which is exactly why when you receive
socks for Christmas or a gift you don't like, you shouldn't
fake excitement or pleasure because you're setting yourself up for a lifetime of similar gifts. However, the very
thing you use to reinforce behaviour, to encourage it to
happen again, must be reinforcing for the other person.
For example, I don't drink alcohol, so if you were to thank
me for doing something for you by sending me a case of
Champagne, it wouldn't actively encourage me to repeat
that behaviour. If you gave me book tokens, however, I'd
be all over you like an aggressive rash.

So, if you're looking to encourage people to do more of
something, or repeat a behaviour, it is essential that you
find out what it is that they find reinforcing. You might
want to reward the team who complete the most sales, for
example, and you might think that an all-expenses trip
to Las Vegas would be flashy, attractive and reinforcing
enough to encourage everyone to pull out all the stops
and perform over and above and then to sustain that for
the benefit of the company. As glitzy and attractive as a
trip to Las Vegas may be, it might not be as reinforcing

for someone with children as having a half day off work, so that they can pick their children up from school and spend time with them, however. Reinforcement is relative, which is exactly why some of us don't need alcohol or heroin. First, find out what motivates, inspires and drives people so that you can reinforce appropriately. Do they eat chocolate or even especially like it? If not, it's a fairly empty gesture buying them a bar to thank them for their efforts.

The same strategy can be used to reinforce ourselves by reserving those things we will work for – the things that we will look forward to, such as a bar of your favourite chocolate, a slice of that cake you made at the weekend or a cup of hot tea, or stopping work early to pick your children up from school. Rather than having these things available all of the time and accessing them whenever, reserve them for when you have completed a task, for example. Reinforcing your focus or hard work with something you enjoy will help you to flip the switch and do more of it.

Feedback and Praise at the Right Time

However, it's not just reward and reinforcement that is so pivotal in changing behaviour, feedback plays an enormous role in our ability to learn not only the most appropriate responses but understand why it is that we choose certain behaviours in the first place. Over the last ten years of working with some of the largest global organizations as a behaviour change consultant, one thing has repeatedly surprised me: the lack of feedback systems in place in nearly all of those organizations. Many of them had customer opinion surveys and some even had staff opinion surveys, but the problem with most of those I've seen is that they run into many pages with very poor, if any, reinforcement for completing them. I'm sure you can relate to starting to complete a questionnaire or survey, with all the best intentions, only to get bored by question eight and resort to just ticking random answers or answering "excellent" for the remaining ones, without any real consideration.

When it comes to helping to change behaviour in order to get the best out of ourselves, and others, it's worth knowing that efficacious feedback loops are continual, not periodical. Think about that for a moment. If you were burnt by an iron just the once, the very first time you touched it when it was on, you would naturally be wary of it and stay away. However, over time, your repulsion would wane and eventually you would accidentally brush past it or catch your arm on it as you manipulated the clothing you were ironing. If you were not burnt by that iron regularly, every time you touched it, your understanding of when it was safe to touch it and when it wasn't would be disrupted because of the inconsistent and unclear feedback you received.

Consider a child at school: they are praised for putting in extra effort and really trying to complete all of the work in their maths class, but they find maths difficult and struggle to perform at the level of the rest of the class. The teacher praises the child for putting in the effort, writes an encouraging comment in their exercise book and completes the praise with a sticker of a gold star. The child feels positive and is motivated to really concentrate and try their hardest again; only the next time, the teacher ignores their efforts: no praise, no written comment – no gold star. No feedback at all is worse than little feedback because the individual is left to work out why there was no feedback: perhaps their best efforts were not good enough? But they really, really tried. In which case, they may as well not bother because if their best efforts receive the same feedback as their minimum efforts, why put additional time and effort in? This is why debriefing, regular review meetings and staff appraisals can be so effective if done correctly because they provide ideal opportunities for feedback and this feedback helps us to fine tune our behaviours and select those which are likely to be more effective in achieving specific consequences.

However, very often businesses will conduct employee engagement or feedback surveys once a year, if at all. The surveys are lengthy and take time to create, distribute, collate and analyse. The results from such sparsely collated feedback become less and less valuable the longer it is between each request for feedback and the more work the organization has to do in order to attend to suggestions for improvement, changes or staff issues. If more organizations better understood the importance of regular, binary feedback systems and the positive behavioural impact that increased frequency of reviews of behaviour, systems and processess can have, over time they would create environments where feedback becomes almost continual: a smooth, flowing system of feedback being proffered, received and readily acted upon, rather than bottled up waiting for the annual "moan sheet".

For optimum effect, feedback could be received as regularly as quarterly, but be succinct in its presentation, rather than saving up lots of questions and requesting opinions and information from a wide cross-section of areas of the organization. By focusing on just a few specific aspects in each survey, the length is reduced, which makes creation and completion much easier and less time consuming; the quality of responses is likely to increase and it will have a positive impact on morale as staff opinions and ideas are sought more regularly. There's more, too: frequent reviews of our behaviours, systems and processess, for example, allow us to act much faster and potentially more easily, with less to analyse and implement. I can't help but think that one-off or annual reviews are just lip-service; but either way, they certainly make it much more difficult for the organization and aren't nearly as effective as regular reviews.

The Importance of Purpose

While my Mum was in High Wycombe Hospital more than thirty years ago, giving birth to me, my Grandma was walking down the hill that their house was built on. As an allegedly chubby child, Grandma would often take me to the vast expanse of green park opposite their house, to kick around a ball in her attempt to get me exercising. However, she continued to bake the most delicious cakes. As Grandma was walking down the hill, she was struck with a crippling pain, which she described as feeling like labour pains. Unbeknownst to anyone at the time, it was at the same time that my Mum was giving birth to me.

Fast forward over thirty years and as I was getting ready yesterday morning, I plugged the iron in, about nine o'clock in the morning. I thought of my Grandma and the sadness I would feel when she passes away from what must be an incredibly isolated life when so imprisoned by dementia. My mind was consumed with thoughts of her lying in her bed, now unable to communicate very well, not eating or drinking and being turned every two hours by staff at the care home she is in to avoid pressure sores. Her character gone. Her personality gone. Her smile and her laughter all but gone.

I remember at the time thinking it was a somewhat random and intense thought to be triggered by plugging an iron in. Almost an hour later, while I was sat at my desk, my Mum called with news of my Grandma's death. She had died at almost exactly the same time I thought of her.

Her death has left a wake of devastation for me and I am sure for her children, too. I loved my Grandma dearly. Now that she has gone, it makes this book so much more poignant.

If we were more consciously aware of how limited and precious our time alive is, I believe we would achieve more with our lives and be more positive, driven and fulfilled as a result of that consciously active drive. My Grandma used to tell people that grass would never grow around my feet. She was right. I don't know why I have accomplished so much with my life but when people suggest that I should slow down, or do less, I remind them of just how short life is. When did you last see a member of your family, or a certain person in your phonebook? Six months ago? Eighteen months ago?

Time flies and we never get that time back, so why on earth would I want to only do one thing or "take a break"? I have only seen a tiny amount of what the world has to offer. I have met just a sample of its inhabitants and come into contact with a relatively insignificant amount of just what is possible. It is time to stop putting things off and live the life you deserve to live and the one that you have the potential for, because when that time comes for all of us, I would hate for it to be full of "what if" and "if only". Regret gnaws at us until we do something about it but for many it is left too late. As Emily Bronte so succinctly put it: "remorse is the poison of life".

6

Make Simple Changes

....

"Everyone is a genius. But if you judge a fish on its ability to climb a tree, it will live its whole life believing it is stupid."

Albert Einstein, theoretical physicist

One of the fascinating things about researching this book, and indeed of human behaviour generally, is the seemingly common belief that in order to change our behaviour, the process must be complicated. While in reality the simplest and sometimes smallest of changes can produce the most astounding and significant results; it is as though we don't want to believe that the stuff that makes us who we are is actually quite simple to alter. If something as common place and yet so technologically advanced as a personal computer, or even smartphone, is complicated, technically speaking at least, then surely a human being is at least as much, if not more, complicated?

The reality is, we can make simple changes to how we think and behave and enjoy significant benefits. Have you ever been in that position where you're driving along a road and someone does something incredibly stupid: they overtake on a blind bend on a dark, snowy night or perhaps they cut you up on the motorway, having only just undercut you. Your innate response to this may well be to flash your lights, or sound your horn, to which they respond by slamming on their brakes, or waving their fist at you or giving you the international sign for "I'm perturbed": the middle finger.

If we instead consider responding differently to what would be expected in any given situation, it is easy to understand, using the example of the car journey, that the consequences could well change things for the better.

Thinking about Walt Disney's quotation that I mentioned at the start of Chapter 1: "happiness is a state of mind; it's just according to the way we look at things", reminds me that most of our emotions are merely a state of mind. We can choose them, or at the very least choose the ones that we want to see through when the most appropriate one is not that we first respond with. This is especially poignant when you consider that our behaviour can be directly affected by the emotions, which we choose, and that it is in itself such a simple change to make. It is possible to give birth relatively pain-free through meditation or hypnosis; and when faced with a crisis which requires our attention or skills, we are able to quickly banish any feelings of panic and fear in order to help. Similarly, some people decide to be religious extremists or racist and others don't. Surely, then, everything is simply a state of mind, not just happiness? We have quite a remarkable ability, as humans, to control and manipulate our emotional responses, sometimes subconsciously – unique to the mammalian world, as far as we know.

Is Changing Our Behaviour Simply Acting?

Imagine an actor who wakes up late for work. He's flustered, and in rushing around to quickly get ready, trips over the cat and twists his ankle. During his frantic showering antics he gets shampoo is his eye, and in a desperate yet temporarily blind attempt to claw it out, knocks his elbow on the tiled wall of the shower. As he's driving to the theatre, he receives a telephone call from his girlfriend, which he takes hands free of course, to inform him that the cat is very unwell and needs to be rushed to the vet and that, while she's on the line, she's going to end their relationship. He finally arrives at work and despite all of this, manages to perform the role of a happy lottery winner to a packed out paying audience.

How does the actor achieve this? How does he behave in such a way that you believe he is the happiest man alive, having just won a huge sum on the lottery, when in reality he is having quite possibly the worst day of his life? He flips the switch.

By playing the part of the lottery-winning man, the actor experiences some of the character's emotions, too, and temporarily suspends his sadness. It's almost as though he has control of a light switch that enables him to turn on an emotional response via the process of distraction.

Actors are not unique in this: we are all capable of changing our mindset and switching our emotional response by looking for simple things to change. One of my friends told me of the time that he wanted to take a day off work; although I'm sure that you wouldn't for a second consider this, it does demonstrate how the same principle an actor uses is something that we all do quite frequently but perhaps without even realizing exactly what we are doing. My friend called into work, making sure that the television and radio were off. His children were already strapped in the car ready for their day at Alton Towers.

Dialling the work telephone number, he strained his voice, doing his best to sound upset, bored, unwell and reserved, all at the same time: "Julie? Hi, it's Keith. Do I? Do I sound that bad? Well I feel it to be honest. I don't think I'll be able to make it in today; I just need to go to bed and try to rest. I'm so weak. I had to get Carol to dial the number for me. What's that? No, I don't think it's terminal – probably one of those twenty-four hour bug things. I hope. Yes, I'll call you in the morning. So sorry, Julie. Thanks for understanding. Apologize to the team for me will you? I'll make myself a Lemsip and think of them while I'm trying to pull through. Okay, thanks – bye." He carefully replaced the receiver, grabbed his keys and got into the car shouting: "Okay kids, let's go! Who wants to go on the roller coaster first?!"

While sometimes it's as simple as thinking "how could I approach this differently? What alternative ways are there to respond?", we can equally benefit from remembering that it's the simple changes we're looking for and not necessarily something complicated that requires much effort or thought.

We Flip the Switch Now, Without Being Aware

Those in management and leadership positions are required to flip the switch overnight when first promoted. I work with a lot of management teams and those in leadership roles and the vast majority of them agree when I suggest that their journey into management was sudden and not necessarily planned. Very often, it turns out that they were very good at something else; maybe sales, or logistics, or IT even. Someone, normally their line manager, spotted potential in them and they were promoted. They might have had some management training internally and been given a manual – which the majority admit to me to have never read in its entirety. Then, overnight, they go from superstar salesperson to manager and are expected to know the answers asked of them by those in their charge; to be able to exude an air of authority and trust and to forge teams, leading and inspiring them to deliver.

If they were honest with themselves, they'd admit that they feel as though they lack the confidence and skills to be an effective leader – and as a result, most have sought out additional books on management and leadership like *Who Moved My Cheese?* in an attempt to fill the gaps. It suggests something about the state of training and development in many organizations. However, they, like actors and like my friend who skived off work to take his children to a theme park, are able to select their behaviours and plan the consequence.

They may not be aware of exactly what they are doing but this is just how frequently we do flip the switch, in many cases to protect ourselves by behaving in such a way that isn't quite our real selves. It's the simple act of pretending almost, acting in the role of a leader, that allows them to fulfil the role, at least from the point of view of presence and outward appearance. The simple change of thinking or acting in the way you wish to be perceived affects our own behaviour and influences that of those responding to us, too.

I'm not suggesting that simply thinking about something causes it to happen. I do not believe that to be so and there is little scientific evidence to support some of the fanciful claims that suggest this. While visualization and projection are important and have been shown to work, there are certain conditions that permit or prevent their success. We have quite a remarkable ability to willingly change our emotional responses to events in our lives. However, many people struggle to change how they think about things because our opinions, carved out of a certain way of thinking about or positioning things within our mind, have elicited an emotional response linked to that behaviour for so long and have created a strong mnemonic. It is this deeply rooted emotional connection that drives our behavioural choices.

Just like practical choices, though, our emotional choices are subject to habit, too. People so passionately believe in certain things that they lose the ability to critically rationalize or, even worse, develop an opinion about something, which they know little to nothing about, as a result of their emotional response to it. While it does take some conscious effort to change the way you think about something, the key to changing your mindset and how you approach this is firstly to remove perceived barriers and obstructions, which would otherwise prevent you from doing this; and, in itself, this is one of the key differences between those people who deliver ordinary and extraordinary things.

While that may sound complicated, remember that where we lack knowledge or understanding, we grow to fear and reject the very thing we do not understand. And in time we grow to hate it. So now, I'm going to offer seven simple changes you can make and apply to every situation in order to help you to flip the switch.

1. View "Problems" as "Challenges"

When presented with an obstacle or problem, extraordinary people do not give up – they do not perceive the obstacles as "problems". Instead, simply "challenges". Consider for yourself when you say the word "problem" where that word appears, or resonates, in yourself. Now compare that to saying the word "challenge". For most people, the two words have different emotional connections and will feel different, perhaps resonating in or being placed in a different part of your mind, or your body, physically.

I once met a lady who whenever she thought of something as problematic would experience anxiety-induced physical symptoms, such as sweaty hands and a flushed face, caused by an increase in her heart rate. Whereas a perceived challenge made her smile and resonated with her competitive, sporty character. When I was studying behaviour, my professor made it clear that if we approached him with only problems, he would send us away with the same problem. "However," he would whisper in his gentle tone, which had a magical quality of intense wisdom to it, "if you come to me with a problem and a possible solution, I'll buy you a coffee and we can explore the solution."

So literally change your language – think no more of problems but of barriers or challenges. Aim to take the same approach to any challenge or barrier you come up against: don't complain and wallow in the negative, focusing on the obstructions; fix it instead. Find a solution, even if at first it is to simply navigate the presenting challenge, in order to get you back on course to your original goal.

If something presents as a challenge, it simply raises a question: "What do we need to do in order to achieve this?" This simple philosophy helps to turn any challenge into a solution, helping to trivialize those things you perceive to be obstructing you.

Perhaps, because I questioned everything as a child (I was the one who always asked "why?"), I have developed an ingrained determination to discover ways to make things happen. If I am told something is not possible or am told the answer is "no", immediately I want to know how we can make the answer "yes" or what needs to be done in order to achieve what we initially set out to do.

Conversely, many people will often accept the very first barrier or challenge they are faced with and then begin to qualify the argument for not continuing, justifying their current behavioural choices; they'll say things like: "well, it will probably take too long anyway", or "it's obviously not meant to be", or even worse, "it's just too much effort to get over those problems". Instead of just accepting this then, change your response to: "What do we need to do in order to make this happen?"

Watch Your Language

Language is so critical to the way that we think and sub-sequently how we behave that there are many books written entirely on that one subject. I present a two-hour lecture about the word "can't" and its limiting repercussions on our behaviour. It's an especially damaging word to use around children but can be equally debilitating for adults. The language that we use, whether it is as part of our internal dialogue or when communicating with others, frames so much of how we think – what we think, why we think it and in turn how we behave or respond to the behaviour of others – that its influence cannot be underestimated. Research has shown that, for example, negative phraseology can prevent us from achieving the very thing we set out to achieve and, conversely, positive language can assist us in achieving it quicker. Try it for yourself. It takes a little getting used to, as the automatic reaction is to offer reasons why something cannot be done, but stop yourself and start the response with: "Yes, if ... "

! NOW FLIP THE SWITCH!

Try this: the next time you're asked a question, instead of automatically responding with "no, because ... " and justifying why it cannot be, find the gap, pause and respond with "yes, if ... " and in place of excuses for why it cannot happen, offer suggestions of how it could happen. This is normal practice in my office; in fact I sit underneath a huge sign which reads: "No, because ..." which is crossed out and underneath is written: "Yes, if ...", as a constant reminder to everyone to consciously flip the switch and find alternative ways to achieve in order to be mindful of how much control we have of the consequences that shape our futures.

2. Ask the £1,000,000 Question

If the barriers are very real, however, and you are faced with a more serious or permanent problem, a different, yet strikingly simple, question to ask yourself is: "if someone gave me one million pounds to do this, would I – or could I – do it?"

If the answer is "yes", then it's clearly an obstruction that can be overcome; it's just that you either do not want to or will not. Perhaps procrastination is playing a part. I use this "million pound question" regularly, to help myself and others get things done that are important.

Some people will take my challenge personally and tell me that they are not doing something not because they don't want to or won't but because they need money in order to achieve it, for example. In some cases this will be true. However, more often than not, in almost all circumstances, it is simply not the case because if we really wanted something, if our lives depended on it, we would stop at nothing to achieve it.

According to waterfortheages.org, the average distance walked by women and children in Africa and Asia in order to get water is almost four miles. They then make the return trip carrying up to 20 litres of water. If you needed it, if you wanted it bad enough, you would do whatever it is no matter what prevents you. However, my point is not a personal one; it's not a pointed attack accusing you of being lazy, dear reader – it's a behavioural one.

Asking yourself the £1,000,000 question is a really simple and quick process that helps to focus your mind by prioritizing the choices you make. Sir Ken Robinson, the education consultant on the arts, widely known for his perfect speeches at the popular TED conferences, once spoke about when television was launched in America.

According to Sir Ken, those in the radio industry warned that this new television invention would never catch on. Their reasoning was that the good, hardworking people of America were simply too busy to sit around all day watching television. At least with radio they could listen and actively work at the same time. Only, they did find time. Lots of time. On average, Americans watch just over five hours of television every day. There are still the same twenty-four hours in the day, but they carved out the time to just sit and watch. Presumably certain things stopped being done or were put off in order to support their new viewing habits.

Every day we are faced with this challenge of doing something or putting it off. It would appear to be a simple enough, harmless choice to make. However, despite the fact that the choice itself is only the first part of the process, this is where many people end their consideration. All the time we are focused on making choices – from the more pathological "what shall we have for dinner tonight?", to the more serious "should we proceed with this deal?" – the consequences, the repercussions of making that choice, are worth much more consideration than we tend to spend on them.

3. Remember the Sum of the Whole is Greater Than the Individual Parts

When it comes to behaviour, very often the sum of the whole is greater than the individual parts. That is to say that what some may deem insignificant behaviours – small things that you assume will not make a difference – when combined with more of those smaller behaviours, often create greater results than would be expected from making only the small changes on their own.

For example, many of the people who ask to work with me in my private coaching programme have previously found themselves quitting activities very quickly. At the first sign of a challenge, they give up. From meeting hundreds of thousands of people all over the world each year, the ability to make small changes is one of the key things that separates those who exceed their own expectations who are readily able to flip the switch and choose more productive behaviours.

One of the ways to ensure you're building all the time on the right behaviours is to employ the simple technique of "stacking". The application of the technique itself yields great results but the change in mindset that is created by understanding the principle is also responsible for great results, directly and indirectly. If we have an idea, why keep it to ourselves? Why not share it with everyone? That freedom of implementing ideas and improvements in the way that we behave is just what helps to make the principle of stacking so powerful. Let me explain how it works.

In England there is a lingerie shop called La Senza. I am reliably informed that Marks and Spencer (another trusted English institution that is as much part of our national heritage as cricket, tea and bowler hats), manufacture especially good underwear. If you were to buy your knickers from Marks and Spencer, you'd walk out with them in a plastic carrier bag, fulfilling its purpose perfectly. However, if you were to purchase your smalls from La Senza, they'd be packaged up in a cardboard bag, featuring coloured rope handles. Your goods are placed inside and then tissue paper placed into the bag, along with aromatic beads and, finally, the whole thing is finished off with a La Senza sticker, used to seal the bag.

Of course, it's all retail theatrics to make your purchase feel that little bit more luxurious and your experience all the more special, helping to close the sale. However, if your lower protective garments were only placed into the cardboard bag, without the tissue paper and other elements, it wouldn't have quite the same impact. If you were to buy your underwear and it was wrapped only in tissue paper, it would be a nice touch but not all that special on its own.

It is the multiple touches; the special bag with rope handles, the tissue paper, the aromatic beads and the sticker, when stacked together, which create the greater, longer lasting effect. The strategy is used all the time in retail and is what Disney refer to as "plussing the show": refusing to believe that anything is truly finished and perfect, instead asking: "how can we make this even just a tiny bit better?" However, you don't often see the principle used in behaviour, which, I think, is a real shame because it's equally as powerful in my experience. The only rule to bear in mind is a simple one: nothing is too insignificant to be stacked. Off the back of your seemingly simple or benign, idea, someone else gets inspiration, and from that another idea is born from someone else and before long, you create something as special and with as much impact as the La Senza packaging. But only if that very first idea is actually put into practice.

 NOW, FLIP THE SWITCH!

Start With a Single Step

What one thing could you put into place that would improve, even a tiny amount, your efficiency at work; the office morale; get you closer to your sales target, or improve customer service; or make life at home less stressful, for example?

What small additional effort could you make toward a happier marriage, enhanced patience with your children or greater self-confidence?

As the Chinese philosopher Laozi so famously wrote: "a journey of a thousand miles begins with a single step".

The length or distance of the journey isn't important; it's what we do on that journey that matters most and it could be something as simple as writing a note to remind you to do something, or spending some quality time with your children, for example, that helps to prevent you forgetting.

As a result of that one tiny thing that you implement, you might decide to schedule more of the important things in your life so as not to forget them and have to deal with the guilt, stress and extra work that often arises when we forget to do things of importance.

4. Apply the +10% Principle

Many years ago, one drizzly evening in Upminster, in the function room of a social club, I met Barrie Richardson, a retired teacher, university professor and amateur magician. A charming, warm-hearted man with a spectacular ability to tell stories and clear metaphors, it was Barrie who taught me the +10% Principle. I have lectured on the +10% Principle for nearly ten years and applied it to every area of my own life. Before we get to how to apply it, let me explain what it is and how it works.

The biggest obstacle for most people when aiming to improve something they do or starting something new is procrastination, often because of an intimidating target. We might want to lose 8 stones but when you have only lost 1 pound at the end of the week, your 8 stone target seems like a lifetime away and so, with dwindling motivation, your attention and dedication to your target wains.

It is the same when revising for an exam or reading a large book: we are not especially good at focusing on the positive things; the weight you have lost or the amount you have read, or the closer you are to your sales target, for example.

However, our species is especially good at focusing on the intimidating chasm between where you are now and where you want to be. But if you were to practise the piano just ten percent more than you do currently, your playing would improve. If you aimed for just a ten percent uplift in sales, it could mean a huge difference to your bottom line. Likewise, a ten percent reduction in costs or waste could make a huge difference, too. It could well be the solution to preventing redundancies.

Ten percent is such a tiny, almost insignificant, amount, that it is easily overlooked. After all, in most other areas, ten percent is ignored. Certainly in sales or in discount offers, we are more interested and attracted to fifty percent or seventy-five percent; even twenty-five percent sounds more appealing than ten. The days of ten percent attracting anyone's attention are long gone.

When I explain to business leaders that we are going to aim to improve output by ten percent, they often challenge me: "But we were thinking something more like forty percent?" The problem with setting such a huge leap in target when there is no historical behaviour to support it is that so many people fall massively short.

An interesting thing happens when we set ourselves an easily achievable goal: many people don't even attempt to try it because it is almost so obvious that it could be done that it does not provide sufficient motivation to do so. Similarly, if a target or goal appears to be too unrealistically obtainable, we do not attempt that either. One of the secrets to successful goal setting to change our behaviour is to set clearly defined, realistic goals, which could be incremental to a larger goal but can be regularly reinforced, which is why the +10% Principle is just so effective.

As Barrie so eloquently describes: "the difference between being a run-of-the-mill organization and a high-performing one is a small increment". Just ten percent. If you look around you and consider the interactions with organizations you've had recently, how many would you grade as extraordinary or outstanding?

The reality is that most people work for organizations producing average results that deliver average services. Most of us receive an average wage for an average day's work. This is not necessarily unacceptable to us, but few of us or the organizations we connect with are extraordinary. But what if every teacher in your local school vowed to improve just one course by ten percent for the next academic year? What if your local police force found ways to reduce not all crimes, just violent ones, by ten percent? What if your local hospital found a way to reduce laboratory costs by ten percent? What if a leading manufacturing company could cut the production lead-time on just one product by ten percent? What if that manufacturing company was a pharmaceutical company? What if every parent committed to spending just ten percent more time with their children?

Agreeing in principle or with a sentiment that sits well with us morally is one thing. However, when faced with choices, we all behave quite differently and it takes different things for each of us to flip the switch. For example, if a new local bakery opened just down the road from you and it sold freshly baked products that were ten percent better quality and tastier than those sold where you usually shop, would you consider shopping at the new bakery? If the staff at the new bakery welcomed you by your name, were polite and carefully wrapped the goods you bought in an attractive cardboard box, would that make a difference? Would you consider moving your children to a different school if the teaching staff could improve the competence or self-confidence of your children by ten percent? What about if your bank offered you a ten percent better return on your investment than who you currently bank with? Would you change banks?

Just a ten percent difference can make a huge impact. No matter whether a business is large or small, if it lost ten percent of its business and did not replace it, this would have an impact across the board; yet, conversely, most businesses can and readily would handle an increase in customers of ten percent.

Barrie believes that the +10% Principle really comes into its own when combined with Vilfredo Pareto's principle of the vital few. Pareto was an Italian economist and sociologist who discovered that for most manufacturing firms, just a small amount of their inventory, less than twenty percent, accounted for some eighty percent of the total value of their inventory. It's become widely known as the "80–20 principle".

In short, we really don't need to be better at *everything* in order to be extraordinary. High performance is within reach of all of us and being able to set goals that are realistic, and therefore more achievable in the first place, makes it much easier for us to adapt and change our behaviour.

NOW, FLIP THE SWITCH!

Your A B Split Test

You can conduct a split test like this for all manner of things: your personal life, work life or career, a specific business challenge or even your physical health – anything at all really.

A. Grab a piece of paper, or use one of the blank pages at the end of this book.

- At the top of one page, write the letter "A".

- Write down all of the words and phrases that come to mind when you consider where you are in your life right now: financial, spiritual, emotional, physical health, career, psychological, etc. Write down anything that comes to mind that sums up how you feel, who you are, how you think, what you do right now.

- Don't write things that concern your dreams or aspirations – take your time to carefully consider it honestly and just write down what's real right now.

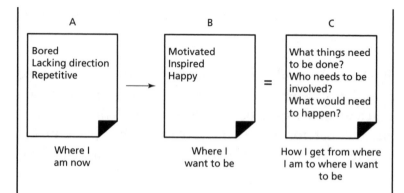

A	B	C
Bored Lacking direction Repetitive	Motivated Inspired Happy	What things need to be done? Who needs to be involved? What would need to happen?
Where I am now	Where I want to be	How I get from where I am to where I want to be

B. Once you've done that, find a new piece of paper and at the top write the letter "B".

- Repeat the same exercise, but this time jot down anything that helps describe where you want to be, where you could be, or need to be, or should be in the future: how do you want to feel?, who do you want to be?, how should you feel?, what do you want to be doing?

- Again, take time to seriously consider this in relation to the different aspects of your life: financial, spiritual, emotional, physical health, career, psychological etc.

- Be honest with yourself – there are no limitations and this exercise is personal to you; no one else needs to see it.

It's important that you start with the first part of the exercise: your "A". Most people are concerned with what could be in their lives but this won't get you any closer to what you aspire to unless you have first carefully considered your position right now. It is this understanding and conscious awareness of our current state that helps us to so simply flip the switch and choose the behaviour with the most appropriate or beneficial consequences.

C. On a third piece of paper, write the letter "C" at the very top.

- This is the part that requires some time, active reflection and an open mind.

- Write the things that need to happen in order to get from your "A" (where you are right now), to your "B" (where you would like to be).

- Ask yourself: What needs to change in my life? What do I need to do more of? What do I need to do less of? Who do I need to connect with or contact?

- Only by setting out clearly what the difference is between "A" and "B" will you be able to clearly define what needs to happen in order to get you there.

I hope that once you've tried this, you'll see just how practical and useful it is whenever you will benefit from clarity and an objective approach in helping to change your behaviour. I've used the A B Split Test with great success with leaders, to help manage the behaviour of those in their charge; it's a useful exercise to help highlight specific behaviours that may be beneficial or obstructive in achieving personal or professional goals, whilst at the same time actively finding solutions to help flip the switch.

5. Avoid Chasing Bigger, Better and Faster

The subject of my talk at the TEDx conference was about our perceptions of generosity and greed and one of the themes I discussed was our seemingly innate desire to chase bigger, better and faster. In reality, we are chasing the positive effects felt from the dopamine release as a result of getting the bigger, better or faster thing, and not actually the thing itself. We are, in effect, chasing the thrill; the buzz we get from the dopamine release as a result of getting the very thing we desire.

Dopamine is the chemical neurotransmitter released into our brain, which associates with happiness and reward. One key point to note is that when we buy something like another pair of shoes, it is not the shoes but the dopamine (and a few other brain chemicals, too) that creates that feeling of happiness and fulfilment which we experience.

We should take note, then, that happiness and fulfilment, the positive feeling we innately chase, can be found in other non-material things, too, which we can find closer to home; those things which we know matter most: our family, our friends and our pets, for example.

A very simple change to make, with potentially life-changing results, is to seek our dopamine fix in things such as these instead. We would not only find ourselves much happier because of our ability to access them more readily, more frequently and more cost effectively but we would also change our brain's neural network, to search in other areas for sources of happiness and fulfilment. Just as we improve our piano or guitar playing skills, or at least hope to improve them, through repetition, changes in how we behave and in our behaviour can be achieved in much the same way. Simply by understanding what drives our behaviour and seeking the stimulus from other sources.

The concept of what we think we become is especially relevant to how we can adapt our behaviour, actions and indeed choices and consequences if we adapt how we think. This raises an interesting point when considering the concept of exceeding our own expectations because perhaps there are other areas where we can seek inspiration and motivation to choose different behaviours that are likely to result in more positive or beneficial consequences. For example, one simple change to consider is that there may be certain friends or colleagues with whom you are less likely to consider your actions and their consequences when in their company. Perhaps in certain situations, or when spending time with family members, you find yourself responding to stimuli in the things they say, the way in which they behave, or the choices they make, for example, and your response is automatic. While it may be automatic, the response may not be the most appropriate or indeed the most desirable.

One of my clients had that exact challenge whenever she had a meeting with her finance director. The two didn't get on and rarely agreed on much, so my client's responses were defensively immediate and not at all considered. On reflection, she recognized that she was often dismissive and argumentative. By paying more conscious attention to the gap between the stimulus (the mere presence of the finance director) and her response, she was able to momentarily pause and better consider her responses, resulting in an almost instantaneously improved relationship. They are unlikely to ever become best friends; however, their ability to work together to achieve positive consequences and even ensure that work life is less stressful and negative for them both is markedly improved. In the gap between stimulus and response lies our ability to flip the switch.

6. Slow Down and Take Stock

Some may argue that the unrealistically perfect ideals presented on social media and on those motivational posters are little more than emotional fluffiness; tools to simply make us feel positive that have little real-world resonance. However, they do offer the opportunity to pause in that gap once in a while; to physically halt the fantastic pace at which we progress and continue through life. They provide us with a moment in time to take stock, and while the messages themselves may not solve world poverty or bring back a loved one, being in the gap just a little longer can help to influence the behaviour that follows.

When people ask me what my favourite activity is or what I enjoy doing at the weekend, I tell them I like to sit on a log, in a field and just look. I watch trees, grass, the sky, squirrels or any other wildlife or elements of nature that happen to be in my vision. Ants are especially nostalgic for me to watch as I'm sure you can now appreciate. Every time I see an ant going about its business, I am reminded of the choices I made that led me to where I am today. Very often people are surprised by this answer and I appreciate that the image of me, the person who runs across auditoriums leaping over the backs of chairs or dangling from chandeliers to help make presentations memorable, instead sits in silence, only watching, while at the edge of a field, is quite a contrast. In fact, the idea of "looking at trees" in your spare time is probably bordering on the need to be medicated.

Technology is developing at a fantastic rate and with it comes the pressure for our behaviour to keep up. We are being encouraged to interact and respond at an increasingly rapid rate, which we are not used to and is a detriment to our ability to find the gap and consciously choose the right responses. It's a very simple change to embrace these timely reminders, which surround us, if only we become more aware of that gap, which is often eroded to become almost non-existent. By slowing down and pausing, we can better appreciate just how in control of our future we are; indeed we can use that time to better control our future.

The little things that make a big difference surround us every day. For the family whose mother or grandfather passed away in their sleep last night, the fact that you woke up this morning, something which you had absolutely no guarantee was going to happen and no biological control over, suddenly becomes more poignant. The smashed car window pales into insignificance when you realize that someone with a terminal illness would gladly swap it for your broken window. Seeing your child walk into the room is something the couple whose child was stillborn long for every second of every day. Even the fact that you can read this book, appreciate the vivid colours and mass of visual complexity the world, your garden and the faces of your friends and family is something that is worth reflecting on and appreciating. According to Action for Blind People, around 360,000 people are registered blind or partially sighted in the United Kingdom[1] and nearly half of those people feel moderately or completely cut off from people and things around them.[2] That alone makes me appreciate just my eyesight, let alone my myriad other capabilities.

Discovering that we have the ability to flip the switch and learning how to pause before response has allowed me to appreciate that.

7. Find a Reminder to Flip the Switch

Life is not just about being grateful for what we do have but is about being able to put our lives and what happens to us into perspective, too. The truth is that despite whatever is happening in your life, right now, you are probably not doing just a little bit, but a lot, better than many other people in this world. I think lists that you often find on social media and on the internet, of reasons to remain positive or reasons to smile or be thankful when you wake up in the morning, are worthy of being printed out and pinned above desks, or framed in hallways or pasted onto the sides of buses or billboards. They offer such strikingly simple, some may argue obvious, advice yet we just don't remind ourselves of it often enough.

---

[1]Access Economics 2009. Accessed online: https://actionforblind people.org.uk/about-us/media-centre/key-statistics/.
[2]Nyman, S. R., Gosney, M. A. and Victor, C. R. (2010) Emotional well-being in people with sight loss. *British Journal of Visual Impairment*, 28, 3, 175–203. Accessed online: http://jvi.sagepub.com/content/28/3/175.abstract.

Most people live their lives every day as it comes: one step in front of the other. When you feel yourself on the edge of a meltdown because your daughter has taken a felt tip pen excitedly to the wallpaper, reminding yourself that you woke up and were able to choose the clothes you are standing in and that you have not feared for your life today, or that you had the opportunity to see the sun rise (you were, admittedly probably still asleep), not only puts the challenges you are faced with into perspective, but makes it much easier to flip the switch and choose your behaviour. Perhaps your choice would be a more positive, calmer response?

I'd like to share with you now one of my own reminders, which I have printed out and stuck to my wall. It is attributed to Robin Sharma and it reads:

The Rules for Being Amazing[3]

Risk more than is required. Learn more than is normal. Be strong. Show courage. Breathe. Excel. Love. Lead. Speak your truth. Live your values. Laugh. Cry. Innovate. Simplify. Adore mastery. Release mediocrity. Aim for genius. Stay humble. Be kinder than expected. Deliver more than is needed. Exude passion. Shatter your limits. Transcend your fears. Inspire others by your bigness. Dream big but start small. Act now. Don't stop. Change the world.

Reproduced with permission of
Sharma Leadership International Inc.

---

[3]Sourced from http://www.robinsharma.com/blog/11/the-rules-for-being-amazing/.

I wish I had written that. It is poetic and almost perfect. It is succinct and covers most of what being amazing would require, I think. The words amazing and extraordinary are often used interchangeably, at least colloquially, however their real definitions are actually quite different. Sometimes all we need is a simple reminder that we can be better; we can try harder; what we believe is as important as what we do and the simplest of things are often the most effective. We each need to find a reminder that we are indeed able to flip the switch.

My reminder is Adam Marshall; a 32-year-old friend from school. Cheeky, musically gifted and with a really deep passion for living life to the full and enjoying every moment. However, in 2014 I attended his funeral. A scan the previous year had revealed two tumours in his brain. I remember well the two occasions that I cried: once when looking at a photograph taken of him and his wife; the picture-perfect couple. And again when his wife walked to the front of the service, holding the hands of their two young sons. Your reminder that we can flip the switch doesn't have to be as sad as mine; however, it should, where possible, be poignant, to help stave off procrastination and put your current circumstance into perspective. You don't necessarily need to find an example that shocks as one that resonates may be more effective.[4]

---

[4]Brain tumours kill more children and adults under the age of 40 than any other cancer. Despite this, just one percent of the national spend on cancer research is allocated to this devastating disease. Adam's family support the charity Brain Tumour Research: www.braintumourresearch.org.

7

Redefine Your Comfort Zone

....

"The most wonderful thing in the world is somebody who knows who they are and knows what they were created to do."

Bishop T. D. Jakes

Stop Thinking – Start Doing

The principles set out in this book work. I know that because not only do I apply them every day myself but so do thousands of others all around the world who I've presented them to or lectured to over the past ten years. However, reading this book could be a fantastic waste of your time if you do nothing with the principles.

What I'm most interested in is what makes us do the things we do. Why is it that some people seem brilliant at their job? Can that energy and apparent magnetism be learnt? How is it that some people's ability and behaviour can be so intrinsically different to that of our own – or of others? Is there a special something that makes people do extraordinary things, or gives them the ability to be better at something than they are currently? I believe so. Which is just as well, otherwise this book would not only have been incredibly short, but fantastically unfulfilling, too. Much like those tiny chocolate eggs that turn out to be hollow. Chocolatiers can be a cruel, cruel group.

To fully appreciate the finer mechanics of the reasons for behaving as we do, we first need to understand the very basic foundations of behaviour. We know that our behaviour produces consequences, and of course those consequences can be good or bad, positive or negative. However, before the behaviour even happens, an antecedent triggers the behaviour. If you like, antecedents cause behaviours to happen. For example, you might punch someone and as a consequence they get a bloody nose and you, quite rightly, end up in the comfortable surroundings of a police car. Before you punched them though, something happened to cause you to throw the punch. Perhaps you had an argument that got heated and out of hand: that was the antecedent.

An example that is hopefully more realistic might be that perhaps you began eating a lot more high fat content foods and, as a consequence, you put on more weight. However, before you started eating burgers, chocolate and ice cream, your beloved hamster, Hammy, died, and left a seemingly irreparable empty hole in your life. Until about three months later when you bought another one: that was the antecedent. So, antecedents happen prior to the behaviour because behaviour doesn't just happen on its own: it is caused. For many people I've spoken to who had no knowledge of learning theory or behaviour, the fact that behaviour is a three-step process, not a two-step one, is quite a revelation.

The chain of an **Antecedent**, which prompts a **Behaviour**, which in turn results in a **Consequence** is often referred to as the 'ABC of behaviour' for, I hope, obvious reasons. In many cases, understanding our behaviour, its likely cause and its subsequent control, is as simple as A, B and C, even though behaviour is almost never easy. In those three

REDEFINE YOUR COMFORT ZONE

letters – A, B, C – we glimpse an insight into why our dog pulls like a steam train when heading towards the park: the consequence to his pulling is that you continue walking closer to the park, thereby reinforcing his behaviour with the greatest doggy reward of all – play at the park. Before the pulling behaviour began, you put the lead on, getting him excited, and then let him pull.

We get a greater understanding as to why a particular child in class may demonstrate challenging behaviour: there are myriad explanations but understanding that the focus shouldn't be on the behaviour itself but on its cause and doing something to prevent the behaviour before it happens or at least escalates, encourages us to approach the situation differently. Why some days are we are irritable and argumentative: perhaps we didn't go to bed early enough the night before and we are running on insufficient sleep. Simple? In essence, yes. Certainly simple enough to take a moment to consider any of your own behaviours and those of others that particularly stand out, and then to reflect on what the antecedent may have been. The bottom line is that behaviour doesn't just happen, and if we can prevent the behaviour from appearing in the first place, it's often a better solution to changing or influencing the consequence than punishing the behaviour, for example.

Why Prison isn't an Effective Punishment (and what it has to do with you)

If I told you what the current reoffending rate was in England, you might be quite surprised. By reoffending rate, I mean the percentage of people who are convicted of a crime, serve a prison sentence and yet despite that punishment, reoffend. At the time of writing, according to the government's own website, fifty-eight percent reoffend in less than twelve months of being released from prison.

So, why do such a significant amount of people seemingly not learn their lesson? Fifty-eight percent would suggest that something isn't working. And it isn't. A revolution in the justice and punishment system is needed and it needs to involve psychologists and behaviourists to advise on the actually quite simple reason why so many reoffend. I'm not suggesting that this isn't a complex issue, which invariably is impacted by budget cuts, staffing challenges and a plethora of other political issues; however, fundamentally, this is about people and changing their behaviour.

What does the judicial system have to do with you? Well, behaviourally speaking, one of the fundamental reasons why so many reoffend is because the feedback they receive for their crime comes far too late. Long-term consequences do not lock into association with behaviour as strongly as immediate consequences do. So if, for example, you were to break into a house – which I'm sure you wouldn't as I like to think that the readers I attract are of high moral standards, intelligent and fantastically attractive too – but let's assume you did and you were caught, you'd be interviewed by the police and kept at a police station until they were ready to bail you, pending a court appearance. That bail period could well be several weeks or months. Eventually you would appear in court and be sentenced for burglary and sent to prison, but your prison sentence could well start many weeks or months after the crime you committed. It's certainly not as immediate or with sufficient enough consequences compared to, say, burning yourself with an iron. And you probably know as well as I do that you have no intention of touching a hot iron again any time soon. Feedback has to be immediate, whether that be a punishment or a reinforcer, to have the best long-term influence on our behaviour and that of others, too.

I have seen many times people attempt to force a change of behaviour on others and subsequently fail. Behaviour cannot be guaranteed. In many ways it would make my job much easier if that wasn't the case and it would make many things in life go more smoothly for all of us. However, this occasional behavioural unpredictability is also one of the reasons that life can be so exciting and is how we benefit from creative output, for example. Sometimes, we simply cannot change others, especially when they do not want to change. As the old English proverb goes: you can lead a horse to water, but you can't make it drink.

Using Our Innate Desire for More

Some of the best pieces of advice in life come from older people. Perhaps obviously, they've been there and done it all. My Grandma used to say to me: "learn from your mistakes". It's easy to get caught up in the day to day tasks of life. The cleaning, family admin or work politics become all-consuming and pull our focus away from our attempts to be better people; but whether it's a note stuck on your computer monitor, a reminder on the fridge, or a bookmark in your diary to remind you: the behaviours we reinforce, we see more of. However, very often there isn't anyone there to reward our efforts, so it's down to us.

It's okay to take time to reflect on the positives, on the things you've done well and the moments you enjoyed. And while, generally, we are relatively good at doing that as we're searching for the next thing – the bigger house, the faster car, the more expensive clothes or the next step up the career ladder – we are not especially good at taking time to objectively reflect on the things that didn't go so well. Some of my colleagues in the behaviour world believe it is a protective mechanism for self-preservation: don't wallow in the negative thoughts because that means we have to deal with them and why try to tackle an emotional crisis when we can just brush it into a dark corner of our brain and move on to something more interesting and positive?

This disassociation is something that neurologists face regularly when treating psychosomatic illness. We tend to deny that it was our fault that something didn't go according to plan, or at the very least we offer a whole package of justifications to comfort and protect us. It is important to bask in the glory of those things that go well but it is equally important to look candidly at those times when we make the wrong choice, or when we don't live up to our own expectations or established morals. It will inevitably be painful but if you flip the switch on that, it is easier to embrace mistakes if they are seen to offer us golden opportunities to tweak and improve for the future; to get different results requires us to adopt different behaviours.

In 1941, Sir Winston Churchill gave a speech to the students of Harrow School. In it he offered this sage advice: "Never, never, in nothing great or small, large or petty, never give in except to convictions of honour and good sense. Never yield to force; never yield to the apparently overwhelming might of the enemy." The international musical phenomenon that is *Oklahoma!* first ran for an epic 269 weeks and grossed over seven million dollars. However, prior to *Oklahoma!*, its writer, Oscar Hammerstein, had five flop shows, which together only lasted six weeks. You might have heard of Admiral Robert Peary, the revered North Pole adventurer? He failed seven times to reach the North Pole, making it on his eighth attempt. Even interstellar travel is considered normal to us now, yet in the first twenty-eight attempts to get a rocket into space the National Aeronautics and Space Administration (NASA) failed twenty times.

There will of course always be individuals who disagree with us and make it their sole life purpose to challenge us or prevent us from achieving what it is that we set out to do. Plenty of people will be there to discourage you and tell you that you can't, shouldn't or won't achieve it. These people are most likely unaware of just how simple it is to flip the switch; to change our behaviour and in turn alter our future through the consequences of our conscious actions – and as much as you may love, care for or respect them, you have the choice, in the gap between their stimulus and your response, to not allow their negativity to stop your journey. This one example is why it was so important for me to explore in this book how alternative ways of thinking can produce beneficial results because, for many, they continue to exhibit the same behaviours. They approach things in the same way and get the same results as they always have done. They allow others to belittle their goals and ambitions with little more than opinion as justification. The comfort and safety that comes with remaining firmly inside your comfort zone and not challenging how or why we arrive at certain behaviours, let alone the consequences we have the ability to alter, drives their very lack of desire to flip the switch.

 NOW, FLIP THE SWITCH!

Managing the Physical Barriers

1 List all the people in your life who are the negative doubters, the naysayers and the pessimists.

Being aware of who they are will help you to prepare for when you have to spend time with them, which is the next part of this quick exercise and worth the few minutes it takes to reflect:

2 How can you best manage those people?

Perhaps you have a choice to spend less time with them? Perhaps you don't but you can avoid certain topics of conversation, or hold back on information that's likely to feed their negativity.

Choosing Mood, Not Just Behaviour

This book is not about our mental health, it is about our behaviour. Given that mental health issues affect 1 in 4 in the UK, is it not important for us to embrace a greater understanding of mental illness? The fragility, the power, the unnerving presence shouldn't be something which we avoid talking about: experiencing mental health issues doesn't mean that you are crazy, in much the same way that needing to wear spectacles doesn't make you blind. It does, however, make you human.

Whether you have or you haven't experienced a chink in your mental health, whether it be diagnosed depression or simply feeling blue, I believe that making a choice over how we let our behaviour impact us and those around us can help not only develop higher performance, but to manage our mood, too. Let me be clear: this does not belittle any genetic or diagnosed mental health issue. I'm not saying that simply changing the way you think will cure you, or even that it's as simple as that to do so in the first place – but our ability to choose our response can be much more powerful than we may think.

The way we perceive something and the opinions we allow ourselves to have on any given matter are flexible. We change, or adapt, readily when we seek knowledge and ask questions. I don't necessarily mean by actively learning or seeking to study in an academic sense, but the act of questioning our own knowledge, our morals and beliefs is key to growing and developing as a person and to achieving extraordinary feats.

Too many take other people's opinions and simply make them their own without question or reflection, for instance. Forming our own opinions instead, based on fact, accurate judgement and knowledge encourages us to engage in activities that will allow us to so much more easily and objectively flip the switch.

The commonality in those individuals who achieve extraordinary things is their ability to think independently; to nurture intrigue and to seek out more knowledge to test their existing knowledge. It's a knowledge Top Trumps of sorts. Having discussed this desire with many people whom I have interviewed, the general opinion seems to be that it comes about because of developing greater confidence in the knowledge and opinions they have.

Developing an opinion about something is important and we live in a free society where we have the ability to do so, which should be embraced and respected. However, by seeking to actively check our opinions, we can be surer of the statements we make, which makes stepping out of our knowledge comfort zones easier to do because, while the results may not be known, the hunch or opinion we have is not simply plucked from thin air, or borrowed from someone we know, but born from our collective knowledge and experiences and the challenging of those things.

Failure to form and check our own opinions simply turns us into clones of other people, and while that wouldn't be altogether that much of an issue if those people had achieved something extraordinary, or had the ability to change their behaviour readily to improve, this is hardly ever the case. As American author Eudora Welty said: "Don't be like the rest of them, darling."

Defining and Redefining Your Comfort Zones

"Do you know there are people who would choose to die in a burning building rather than run outside with their pants off?" the social psychologist Stanley Milgram writes. Presumably he wasn't the one giving them that choice in some bizarre (and frankly cruel) psychology experiment. Living within a psychological and behavioural comfort zone is, by definition, comfortable.

From where our mugs are kept in the kitchen, to our favourite mug for tea and the length of time we leave the tea to brew and then how much milk we add, all the way through to the route you take to work and what you wear to work, all are ingrained, habitual behaviours that form our comfort zones. I once met someone who confided that he not only had socks with days of the week printed on them but that he also had pants into which he'd had his wife sew little labels with the days of the week on. If that wasn't slightly odd in itself, he told me that he felt out of sorts if he wasn't wearing the corresponding socks and pants for that particular day.

Being Emotion Neutral

Comfort zones are so named because the behavioural and psychological area that we naturally like to be in is anxiety-neutral – i.e. one that is comfortable and one we can be at peace with. Not at all like the state you find yourself in when your friend's annoying partner comes round. All of the behaviours that define our comfort zone are boundaries of sorts that we develop over time; things that we decide we are, or are not, comfortable with – that either make us slightly anxious or keep us free from anxiety. In turn, these definitions make us feel safe and secure. Doing something different, such as changing our behavioural response, takes us outside of our defined comfort zones and that is something many people find very difficult to do indeed. It highlights our feeling of insecurity.

Security is a key, innate need of humans. People who live on the Isle of Mann seem to have lived the longest of any Western society I know with so much trust and seemingly innate displays of security. I was on the island for the first time several years ago, presenting to a financial group, and as the taxi driver took me from the airport to the hotel, he gave me a verbal historical tour of "Mann". He'd lived on Mann all of his life and told me that, so tight knit and close was the community on the island that, up until recently, no one locked their front doors. He told me how his neighbour had moved away from the island and a new family from the main land moved into the house, only to be woken the next morning at just gone seven by banging in the kitchen. Fearing an intruder, the husband made his way downstairs brandishing a slipper, presumably intending to attack the intruder with an additional level of comfort, only to find the island's postman in their kitchen. Having duly laid out the family's post on the kitchen table, he was now making himself a cup of tea. Both men were as shocked as each other at the unexpected sights. The taxi driver went on to say how times were changing and that more people were now locking their front doors on Mann, although I was reassured it was not because of the postman.

Actively doing something about how we respond to stimuli, whether it be exhibiting a new behaviour or changing an existing behaviour, changes the set boundaries of our comfort zones. That doesn't come easy for most – and understandably so. It's more than about being "set in our ways" and usually nothing to do with being stubborn, although there are always exceptions. We seem to be aware, all-be-it for many of us subconsciously, of the fragility and complexity of life.

How Our Mood Drives Results

To help combat the uncertainty and feelings of anxiety and self-consciousness we experience when we are without patterns of familiarity, we find ourselves creating them in order to feel safer: driving the same routes to work, reading books by the same authors, setting subconscious time agendas for meal times, shopping or boiling the kettle and cooking the same core meals. And for most of these activities it is subconscious. It's little wonder that so many people struggle to understand just how they can be any different than how they are right now when they are seeking out and surrounding themselves with the same information and repeating similar behaviours. Achieving different results doesn't have to mean a dramatic restructuring of our comfort zones, or reinventing ourselves with entirely new opinions, responses and preferences, like you might see in a mid-life crisis, for example. It can simply be a case of doing the same things but differently: choosing a different route to work to engage your mind with alternative stimuli or to inspire you; reading other authors and seeking information from alternative sources. Perhaps even seeking out different social company.

The result is that these new or altered behaviours help to activate and change the way parts of our brain communicate with other parts and, in turn, this helps to change the way that we think about and approach things. It has long been known that our mood is affected by our environment and especially the music we listen to. Studies have been conducted that demonstrate how listening to upbeat music can increase episodes of road rage in drivers, for example, whilst listening to classical music has been shown, in seemingly endless studies on the subject, to calm mood and promote relaxed behaviours – and yes, to help reduce both the frequency and severity of road rage. Interestingly some studies comparing the effects of listening to individualized music (that is music which the individual would prefer listening to), compared to classical music, have shown that individualized music reduces agitation and distress in those with dementia and cognitive impairment, for example.

All of this really just demonstrates that music is therapeutic and that what suits one person, doesn't necessarily suit another or even have the same impact. However, regardless of the style, if the music we listen to can have such a dramatic effect on our own behaviour then surely it is not such a giant leap of faith to consider that so too can our own decision to change our behaviour. And such is the case. Why sit there wringing our hands, grinding our teeth and puffing our cheeks out while the rapid, boundless notes of Mozart blare out of the speakers, waiting for it to take effect like some junky hit of holistic therapy, when we can actively choose to calm down, react differently and control our behaviour, simply by making the choice to consciously flip the switch?

The Imaginary Can Rule Our Mind

I've worked with thousands of individuals and groups of people, all over the world and from all walks of life, in almost every sector of industry, to achieve things they didn't think were possible. My company's coaching programme helps people to step outside of their comfort zone every single day and the greatest hurdle most frequently seen that holds people back seems to be the mere concept of this protected, imprisoned set of values, which we refer to as our comfort zone.

Just like the notion of root canal treatment, end-of-year exams, driving tests and appointments to see your tremor-ridden proctologist, the somewhat mystical comfort zone gets far too much imagination space than it deserves. All of this talk of doing things "outside of our comfort zone" only helps to exacerbate the problem. I take a very bold line when it comes to zones of comfort or any other – I ban them.

There is no such thing as a comfort zone.

It's a bold statement to make, I agree, and possibly controversial. However, read that last sentence over and over to yourself at least ten times.

All that matters is how we respond to the challenges that present in our lives and to the people we find ourselves with; the environments we end up in and the day to day changes in the here and now. If you ever find yourself feeling anxious about the situation you're in, or about a potential new behaviour, such as a charity bungee jump for example, then remember that the only reason that little feeling of anxiety is present is because you're scared. We fear the unknown because – well, it's unknown. It's a perfectly natural emotion and what has kept our species alive. Pity it has kept so many alive frankly, but there you have it.

The physiological manifestation, the physical feeling, of fear is often identical to that of excitement, however. It is our mind that frames the physicalities as bad anxiety, or conceptualizes them as negative, based on the context. So, if the actual physical changes experienced: elevated heart rate, the adrenaline rush and sense of anxiety, are the same as excitement, could we flip the switch and think about being excited about trying something new, for example, rather than being nervous, anxious and worried? Could we in fact focus on the positive aspects and embrace the new experience, with no thought given to pre-defined zones of comfort?

 NOW, FLIP THE SWITCH!

Choosing Your Emotional Response

You've got a choice, remember: you can jump on the worry train and let that fear take you on a roller coaster so wild and fast that you'll be throwing up the contents of your stomach in no time, or you can choose not to ride.

So, now: choose to ask yourself the following:

- How do I want to feel?

- How do I want to respond to this?

- How should I respond to this?

- What action should I take and what are the consequences of those actions?

The key to change is to let go of fear, and the more dramatic and less controlled you allow a situation to become, the greater the negative consequence on your own behaviour and in turn those that are affected, too.

Deal With What's Real

Deal with what's real – drop what's not. Today it's raining outside. It's overcast and windy and, with the lights off, it's dull and dreary. However, for me it's my favourite kind of day. Light a candle, brew a pot of tea and pop a side light on and my home is magically transformed into a safe haven. As I look out of the large dining room window, I see nature doing what it does best and am thankful to be in the relative warm, my mood lifted by the flickering candle and my cup of tea. It's the simple things that often help us to flip the switch as a behavioural prompt, but the things that help to transform my day from grey to great are the parts that very often I put in place. I've changed how I feel today by taking charge of my environment and that's something not enough of us consider.

I call those people the back-seat moaners because, while other people like me are in the driving seat, taking control of their day and the consequences of their actions, they just sit in the back moaning that it's too cold, or too wet or that they're bored or uncomfortable. Put a jumper on or turn the heating up. Get an umbrella or a waterproof coat, but do something! It's those back-seat moaners that we come across in daily life who have helped shape my mantra of "deal with what's real – drop what's not". Those things that haven't happened yet, or which are inconsequential in the grand scheme of things, are often not worth spending time on; they hold you back and prevent you from spending time and energy on the things that really matter. For example, while you're moaning about being cold, you could be actively doing something about it to change the situation and moving forwards, progressing with your goals or life. Those very same people are often the ones who complain that their friends don't put in enough effort to see them and that can't be coincidence, can it? Doing something about the current situation that you find yourself in, in order to alter the consequences, is the very essence of flip the switch.

It's not just about jumpers and umbrellas though, of course. If we all take a moment to consciously monitor our responses to our environment and our reactions to those around us, in an attempt to catch ourselves spending time or energy on the things that we can actively do something about, we can literally train our brain to be more proactive, whilst simultaneously getting more done, realizing our own happiness faster and being more efficacious in our approach to our work life, home life and personal development.

The things that affect us here and now are the things that we need to deal with; the things that might be, or that we don't have sufficient information to base a sound judgement on yet, or those things that we know little to nothing about, are a waste of time to worry over and spend time on. The "what if" scenario – "what if this had happened?", "what if we had more money?", "what if they hadn't had gone there?" – is very often a waste of time if we can't yet influence the consequence, or if the consequence has already happened. Making a decision or acting upon third-hand knowledge or information from people who won't have all of the knowledge you need, is one of those "drop what's not" moments.

We could spend all of our lives forming opinions, making decisions and acting upon advice based on things that aren't concrete, justified, substantiated – real. I've sat in boardrooms around large tables surrounded by senior executives while time is wasted as they engage in debate about things they don't actually need to concern themselves with just yet, because they are making assumptions and hypothesizing on areas where they lack real knowledge about what might happen in the future. One question normally brings the entire room to a standstill: "Do you need to make a decision on this right now, or can it wait until you have all of the facts?" And so it should be in our own businesses, at home and in our personal lives, too, because as a result we'd be so much more time-rich, so much more focused on the things that really matter and so much more productive, getting closer to our personal and work goals.

! NOW, FLIP THE SWITCH!

But What Will You Do?

As we near the end of the book, I thought it might be worth reviewing what we have done to change:

- What have you highlighted that you need to change?

- What action have you taken on this so far?

- What were the effects of that action?

- What are you going to do about it?

- Setting clear deadlines is important in order to achieve, so when are you going to do this by?

- Will these actions meet your goal?

- Who will you need assistance from in helping to achieve this, if anyone?

8

A Final Reminder to Change

··

"I used to think that the worst thing in life was to end up alone. It's not. The worst thing in life is to end up with people who make you feel alone."

Robin Williams, comedian, actor, entertainer

This Day Shall Be Mine

Alzheimers and dementia are, for many, cripplingly cruel diseases of loneliness, confusion and frustration. However, it doesn't have to be. The excellent work of organizations like the Contented Dementia Trust[1] and their SPECAL method are helping to change the lives of thousands of dementia sufferers to afford them lifelong well-being.

And so it is with our lives; they don't have to be as they are right now. We don't have to be a passenger of the product of what's happened to us in the past and what might in the future. Many people tip toe through life neither confident, nor sure of who they are or where they are going. I wonder if you can relate to that? We do not have to be trapped in a suffocating state of ordinary. Each one of us has great potential and our own individual strengths are others' weaknesses – and vice versa – as demonstrated by so many inspirational examples of the past and present.

---

[1]The Contented Dementia Trust is an independent charitable organization with an innovative approach to the lifelong well-being of people with dementia. www.contenteddementiatrust.org

I believe it is more important for us to find ways to improve or solve the situations that we are in, which will help to make our lives more engaging and rewarding. One question I urge you to ask yourself at least once every three months, is this: *is there anything in my life that I want to change?* You need to articulate those things now, not in four years' time when they've become such ingrained issues that you can't do anything about them. Naturally, some things you won't be able to change; however, you will be able to choose how you respond to them.

So remember, it's up to you to make the best out of the situations you are presented with; to focus on exactly what it is that you want to do more of – or less of – and to ensure you find that for yourself, or indeed create it for others.

Thomas Heath Flood wrote: "This day shall be mine. From the first gray streak of its early dawn till the last golden ray of its setting sun melts away on the horizon of the West, it shall belong to me ... I will live so that should tomorrow dawn, I may look upon today with a feeling that I have added my humble mite to the cause of Justice and Humanity." You could do worse for inspiration to focus your outlook and sense of purpose.

And that is what people really want and I dare say need: purpose. However, it isn't found without challenging why we do what we do. Board members, senior executives and managers all have a duty to help ensure happiness and a sense of well-being in those who work for them, in order to get the best out of their staff and to develop higher performance in them. They have a responsibility to provide them with a sense of purpose. As do we for our children and those we care about.

Selflessly, it is worth considering the implications of the impact on others of our ability and inability to choose the right behaviours. Naturally, we can help others to do the same for those in our charge, colleagues, students, patients and indeed at home. When I'm working with organizations or groups of people I always encourage the practice of hand-writing feedback or thank you notes. They act as a marker for the behaviour if provided close enough to the specific act, or behaviour that you wish to reinforce, and of course they are themselves, for many, a reinforcer in themselves. The impact of hand-written communication is not written about nearly enough and certainly not implemented nearly enough given the positive and beneficial results it produces.

Some of the most effective ways to create change are in fact the simplest, yet often we seek much more complicated ways in the assumption that more challenging or more expensive or more complicated will somehow yield better results. A simple thank you note that could be in a card, or simply on a sticky note stuck to someone's desk, or even better from the CEO or someone with respected authority, which says: "we really value your efforts", "you are making a difference", or "I'm hearing great things about your work" can be enough to help others to choose and maintain the right behaviours.

Why We Don't Change How We Cut Carrots

When we want to change, when there's a genuine desire or need to, it's easy to flip the switch and make that first move. Well, perhaps it's not always easy but it's certainly easier when you have a reason to do so. That caveat of wanting to change applies to others, too: it's extremely difficult to change the way other people respond and behave if they themselves either don't see any reason to, don't believe there is a need to or simply don't want to. One thing that especially makes me smile and at times laugh out loud is when visiting friends for dinner and, while socializing in the kitchen, one of them will be preparing vegetables and their partner will chime in with: "you don't cut carrots like that!" and the subsequent lesson on how to "correctly" cut carrots their way falls on deaf ears. The partner's way of cutting carrots is perfectly functional and has suited them until now, so there's no desire to change. Nor is there likely any need to: julienne or sliced, they all taste like carrot – the end result is ultimately the same.

There are myriad reasons why we don't change our behaviour; however, as I've alluded to before, one of the key culprits for behavioural stagnation is procrastination. We put things off not in an act of laziness, as many assume, but in the hope that if we don't do it, the need to carry out the task will go away on its own. It's an effective strategy in a busy world and of those with a busy lifestyle because many of the things on our to-do lists do go away if we leave them long enough: other people pick up the slack or new projects take the limelight. And it's that mentality of not needing to change that bleeds into our day-to-day behaviours. The world will continue and evolve for the time being if we don't make any attempt to do anything differently and organizations, groups and families will continue to function, many of the dysfunctional examples eking out their days using functional coping mechanisms to continue in place of changing their behaviour.

Procrastination reigns supreme because of a lack of vision; a lack of clear understanding of why the changes need to happen. The vision is almost like a destination in a satellite navigation system because, without knowing exactly where we want to be, we quickly lose any inspired interest or determination to get there. That's why exercises like the A B Split Test are just so useful and why having a clearly considered understanding of why we do the things that we do and the consequences of them is so critical. Procrastination is normal, as are those days we all get when we don't quite have the same level of motivation that we had yesterday. However, perhaps how we respond to that procrastination needs to be extraordinary.

 NOW, FLIP THE SWITCH!

Managing Procrastination

1 Understand "why?" Clearly articulate why you need to do this. What is the end result you're looking to achieve?

2 Consider the consequences. What will happen if you do achieve this, or carry out the desired behaviour? What will happen if you don't?

3 Identify the barriers. What is it that is putting you off? A lack of confidence? Fear? Lack of knowledge or understanding? What do you need to do to correct these?

4 Find help. Seek out people to share your concerns with, help you to flip the switch and change your response to the barriers.

5 Start! The Achilles heel of procrastination is to start doing. Write a list of the things you need to do in order to get to the desired change and in order to provide you with a confident plan to refer to and, starting at the top, get doing them.

"Fear" and "a lack of confidence" are common reasons that people cite for not feeling that they are able to change their behaviour, or the behaviour of others. There are far too many variables to consider in the scope of this book as to what exactly might prevent us from changing; however, both those feelings of fear and a lack of confidence often, in my experience in the context of behaviour change – and for the purposes of this example I'm referring to non-clinical, non-traumatic, non-specialist behaviour change – stem from a lack of knowledge. When we don't feel confident in the knowledge or skills that we possess in order to successfully change, we tend to err on the side of caution, which results in procrastination. We leave those things we don't feel as confident doing until last, perhaps in the hope that someone else will make the decision for us. And then we put them off in the hope that they'll go away on their own. The solution of course is to recognize this and build a separate plan for how to learn, or do whatever it is that you need to do in order to feel more confident. Without the plan to do so, though, the dominant emotion of self-doubt and avoidance of the things we need to do in order to change fuels our procrastination further.

Those are entirely self-imposed reasons why we don't change; however, as I mentioned before, sometimes we need to act when the behaviour of others begins to have an impact on our own. Those external factors that prevent us from changing entirely, or negatively influence our choices, need addressing, too. If nothing is done about the things that influence our behaviour in ways that are contrary to our desired outcome, we begin to forge new, or compound existing, deep habitual behaviours that prevent us from being able to readily flip the switch. Instead we put things off, procrastinate and justify to ourselves why we aren't changing. So what can be done about it? This is the area of behaviour change to which the maxim "it's simple but it's not easy" best applies.

We Tend to Seek the Easy Way Out

We don't respond especially well to being told what to do and bossed around. When people start to lay down the law and tell us how we should behave, laying down rules and regulations, we tend to respond defensively. It's not especially motivating as an approach to changing behaviour, because when we don't feel that we have any autonomy, or our opinions don't count, our willpower muscles get tired much faster. It takes much more willpower to go along with instructions and orders. Inclusivity and suggestions that speak and appeal to people's hearts as well as their brains is how we are going to better engage people and encourage specific behaviour changes.

However, we are all guilty of looking for the easy option in most things in life. We're a species of magic wand seekers; we all want the pill or the diet or even the person that will do the hard work for us: we don't actively work at our marriages or seek knowledge on how to be better parents; we use fear, intimidation and violence in favour of understanding, patience and peace. So it appears much easier to just give people a pay rise and hope that will make them happy instead of taking the time to find out what they find motivating and reinforcing and asking what happens in their job that makes them want to leave. The long-term benefits of behaviour change take consideration and a little more effort and thought to work out. It is those individuals and organizations who recognize the additional effort they put in to regular appraisals, soliciting feedback, developing an inclusive team and seeking out suggestions for ways to improve, that help create a higher performing team who are able to recognize when to flip the switch and exactly how to do it. So, is the key to being able to choose our behaviour, mindful of its consequences and our ability to achieve extraordinary things, simply a case of thinking differently and putting in additional effort?

Clearly it is more than that because applying extra effort to the wrong areas and at the wrong time, for example, would not necessarily yield the desired consequences or indeed extraordinary results. Not allowing yourself to be restricted by what has gone before you and daring to try something different, accepting that you might have been wrong or that it may not work but that the result is not all that tragic in the grand scheme of things compared to the payoff if it works; I don't believe that doing this makes you a maverick, nor does it encourage you to actively go against the grain just for the sake of doing so. It does, however, give you the freedom to decide for yourself that you won't be actively confined to the way others think and behave; be restricted to following the same ideals, methods and ways of working as others and to look bleakly around you and ask, in a hushed and hopeful voice: "Is this it? Is this all there is?"

 NOW, FLIP THE SWITCH!

Never Lose Sight of Reason

Another day there will be a different story to tell and your life will be one more day further on, so don't allow whatever happens today to define your outlook.

While events might flow over to another day or week – or even month, nothing stands still – today's news is tomorrow's history, when tomorrow comes. Every second of our lives that ticks away becomes another minute that passes us by. Every hour that escapes us is another day that disappears and every Christmas that "came around so quickly" is full of both potential memories and opportunities for us to create extraordinary moments.

Don't use other people's positions or progress to judge your own progress: don't measure your chapter one on someone else's chapter twenty-five.

Keep focused on what you are achieving and on that end behaviour you're aiming for.

Oscar Wilde wrote: "To live is the dearest thing in the world. Most people exist, that is all." My experience echoes Wilde's opinion: many more people simply exist and, while that is fine if it is their choice, many of those who only exist in the concept of behavioural choice and consequential influence are unaware that they are doing so. They accept life as it is. A simple series of events: of waking, some activity in the middle where things happen to them, which includes some eating and bodily functions, then sleeping. Then they wake up again and rinse and repeat. We will always have the capacity to make more money but we'll never get any more time.

To this end there are a series of rules you can use to remind yourself to change your response to anything that life throws at you. Take them as they are, or use them as inspiration to create your own:

Did Anyone Die?

This helps me to keep things in perspective. The loss of life is, I'm sure you'll agree, the worst that could possibly happen in any given scenario, so if that didn't happen, I know it could have been worse.

Wings of Steel

This reminds me of just how resilient we naturally are: our coping strategies vary from person to person but most of us have a strong foundation if we spend time creating it.

Set Goals

Without things to aim for and focus on, much of our precious time is wasted. This rule ensures that I set goals in order to then schedule my time to achieve them; it's win–win.

"Yes, If ..."

The language we use helps to shape our behaviour and in turn our mindset.

Understand My Responsibility: Action = Consequence

My behaviour is my responsibility, not anyone else's. This helps to keep me in check whenever I begin to justify that the actions I take and their consequences might not be 100 percent my responsibility.

Experience is Not a Negative

We often allow the consequence to decide the final feeling or result of our behaviours, neglecting the fact that by flipping the switch anything that doesn't turn out as we planned or expected can be accepted as experience in that field or in life itself.

Find a Positive or Learn a Lesson

Not everything can be seen in a positive light. As Zephyr said: "in every white there is a stain". If that's the case, search to learn a lesson so that, in turn, you create something positive for yourself from it. This is invaluable in changing how we approach challenges and let them affect our response.

This Life is For Me

Gentle reminders of why we do the things we do and make decisions and choices that are sometimes just for us are important to maintain balance.

 NOW, FLIP THE SWITCH!

You'll Never Get Any More Time

1 Grab a piece of paper and a pen, or if you can only find a pen or pencil you'll find some blank pages at the back of the book for you to make notes.

2 Consider the following: The average lifespan of an adult male in England, at the time of writing, is 78.9 years for an adult male and 82.9 years for an adult female, according to Public Health England. There are twelve months in a year, which means women will live for an average of 994.8 months and men for 946.8 months.

3 How old are you right now? Multiply your age by 12, to get the number of months that you've been alive so far. (For example, if you're 30, it's 360.)

---

4 Now subtract the number of months you've been alive (in this example 360), from your average monthly life span (I'm a male, so my calculation would be 946.8 – 360).

5 The answer (in this example 586.8) is how many months you have, on average, left to live. It's a sobering thought, isn't it?

When my friend and colleague Terry Gormley first took me through this, I remember thinking just how very real my life suddenly felt. It's your choice what you do with your time but all of those that we've known, loved and lost no longer have that time available to them. But we do. It's our responsibility, surely, to make the most of what we have left?

So what four new habits are you going to adopt to help you to work on finding the gap; becoming more conscious of that space between our stimulus and response and choosing to flip the switch to find the most appropriate behaviour to affect the desired outcome?

Gwendoline Pearl Cunliffe was the perfect catalyst for extraordinary.

Now it's your turn – flip the switch and be extraordinary.

Afterword

In 2007 my life took a monumental change of direction. I found myself sat staring at the plain walls of a small room in the Spinal Injury Unit of Sheffield Northern General following an accident during one of my horse riding competitions. I now had a life-changing burden hanging over me – I was no longer able to walk, let alone compete in any riding events, for the rest of my life.

It's not uncommon to hear that the biggest difficulty someone faces with becoming paraplegic is not just the day-to-day living with being paralysed chest down, but the internal struggle you have with yourself to come back with a fighting determination. It's all too easy to let it defeat you.

It is this exact point that is addressed so beautifully by Jez: how to become great. He makes you realize that by using a few simple techniques you can truly empower yourself by achieving so much more than you ever thought possible. It doesn't matter which extreme you approach it from; whether, like me, you are returning after something like a life-changing accident, or you are making your comeback after a slight dip in your career, through reading *Flip the Switch* you can be extraordinary.

I don't doubt for one second that any reader of *Flip the Switch* has learnt that "being extraordinary" is not just the principal focus of the book, but a fundamental life lesson that can benefit anyone who puts it into action. From here, see how much you can now grow and become the absolute best you can be, even when faced with seemingly crushing setbacks. Although at the time my accident was totally devastating, I have now achieved things I wouldn't have done if it wasn't for that day that changed my life. When I was at school my worst nightmare was speaking in front of the class; now I am a speaker and love it. I would never have believed this. Never say never. Becoming paralysed has made me do things I would have thought were impossible.

The one thing I've learned over the years is that to achieve any goal you set yourself and to really achieve results, you must not only believe in your ability to achieve it, but be prepared. Often, being prepared mentally can be just as, if not more, important than the necessary physical preparation. I was 32 years old (and paraplegic for five of those years) when I decided to take on the immense task of completing the Virgin London Marathon using the ReWalk bionic suit. Yes, it was an extremely harrowing experience physically, trying to walk 26 miles when in reality I couldn't walk at all. But it was the small hurdles that I struggled with the most, like trying to lift my legs over pavements that are often very bumpy and uneven. I took each step of my seventeen day journey as it came in the same way I have done for the past eight years since my accident.

My journey has been tough but extremely rewarding and I know everyone reading this will have embarked on their own extraordinary journey through life – a journey that is subjective and entirely unique to you. Whatever yours is, use the *Flip the Switch* principles to focus, achieve and drive that ambition further each day. Take heed of Jez's invaluable advice and use the book to remind yourself that you really are capable of so much more than you believe you are right now. Try it – be extraordinary.

Claire Lomas[1]
Campaigner, Fundraiser and Speaker.

---

[1]To hear more about Claire's incredible story and her remarkable enthusiasm, listen to her episode of my podcast series, The Extraordinary Podcast, available on iTunes: bit.ly/tepodcast

Helping You To Get Extraordinary Results

....

I've been creating and delivering training programmes and materials to help individuals and organizations to develop higher performance for almost twelve years. In that time I have produced a huge amount of resources on various aspects of business learning and development, including printed materials, video lessons, webinars, infographics, podcasts and articles to help make the greatest impact in your business for just about any industry.

I'm very excited to announce the High Performance Programme; an online portal jam-packed with training resources, especially designed to get extraordinary results from ordinary people.

Head on over to www.HighPerformanceProgramme.com to watch the video and get instant access to thousands of resources to help with your personal and professional learning and development.

Acknowledgements

···

As any author will tell you, usually only one name appears on the cover, yet there are many people involved in getting the book to your hands. Some have direct roles and others help more than they could ever imagine, but indirectly. My executive assistant, Steph Middleton-Foster, I simply couldn't be without; she perfectly manages my diary, which allowed me the time to write this. In the same light, my manager Kenny Donaldson is something of a rare find indeed and I am indebted to his professionalism, support and guidance, ably assisted by Jean. I am very grateful to those who gave up their time to discuss ideas with me or be interviewed for this book: Richard McDougall, Robert Williams, David Goodfellow and Sheila Marshall. Thank you to Robin Sharma for permission to use his *Rules for Being Amazing*. The team at Capstone have been so welcoming and helpful and I am indebted to the sharp eye and mind of my editor, Jenny Ng, and her ability to make sense of my words. Claire Lomas's journey puts a perfect metaphorical full stop to the end of the book – I hope it inspires you to never give up and to look for alternative ways to respond to life's challenges in order to influence your future. I'm not going to list the many friends and colleagues I've met in television, for fear of this reading like a who's who of who's on screen (or not, depending on when you're reading this). However, public thanks must go to John Kaye Cooper, Tony Nicholson, Marc Paul and Tony Humphries for the parts they have played in creating engaging and fun projects for television.

Thank you to my clients across the world for choosing to work with The Behaviour Expert and for embracing positive behaviour change. In some cases those changes have been significant and, such is the nature of behaviour, the process has not always been easy. To see and share with you the results of higher performance is a joy and the core purpose of why we do what we do, so thank you for having that intrigue, belief and taking the leap of faith to do something about it. No matter what I'm doing, my parents almost always get mentioned; their unfailing support and patience cannot be thanked enough. The team at the Contented Dementia Trust, my adopted charitable partner headed up by the inimitable Penny Garner, are tireless, dedicated and constant in their efforts to bring a greater sense of well-being to those living with dementia and their families. I've learnt so much in the relatively short time I've been working with them and never cease to be excited about the SPECAL method and their deep belief in changing the way that those with dementia live. Extra special thanks are reserved for my wife; she is the perfect, patient partner. And finally to you, for your intrigue and for reading this far. Thank you. Now stop reading about people you don't know and begin your journey to extraordinary.

About the Author

Photo credit: Alex Healy 2015

Jez Rose is a behaviourist best known for his humorous and engaging training presentations and as the regular behaviour expert on BBC radio.

As an author, speaker and recognized thought leader in the application of brain science for business, his company – The Behaviour Expert – helps to positively change behaviour for organizations worldwide. His global clients include Old Mutual Wealth, Philips, Volkswagen and Marriott.

Possessing the rare ability to both inspire and offer real-world strategies for change, he has been a featured guest on more than 200 radio and television programmes, including his own sixty-minute special for ITV. His writing has been published in international trade and consumer press, including *Forever Sports* magazine and the *Daily Mail* and *Telegraph* newspapers.

In 2010 he was made a Fellow of the Unite University programme and in 2014 was invited to speak at one of the renowned TEDx conferences. Find out more at www.thebehaviourexpert.com and follow him @JezRose.